W9-AMW-503

BUSINESS BRIEFS

165 GUIDING PRINCIPLES FROM THE WORLD'S SHARPEST MINDS

BUSINESS BRIEFS

RUSS WILD

PETERSON'S/PACESETTER BOOKS

PRINCETON, NEW JERSEY

Visit Peterson's at http://www.petersons.com

Copyright © 1996 by Russell Wild

All rights reserved. No part of this book may be reproduced, stored in a retrieval system, or transmitted, in any form or by any means—electronic, mechanical, photocopying, recording, or otherwise—without written permission from Peterson's.

Peterson's/Pacesetter Books is a registered trademark of Peterson's, A Division of Thomson Information Inc.

Library of Congress Cataloging-in-Publication Data

Wild, Russell.
    Business briefs : 165 guiding principles from the world's sharpest minds /
Russ Wild.
      p.   cm.
    ISBN 1-56079-595-6
    1. Success in business. 2. Career development. 3. Management. I. Title.
HF5386.W496   1996
650.1—dc20   96-16401
                                                                CIP

Editorial direction by Andrea Pedolsky   Cover design by Todd Radom
Production supervision by Bernadette Boylan   Cover illustrations by James Bennett
Composition by Gary Rozmierski   Interior design by Cynthia Boone
Creative direction by Linda Huber

Printed in the United States of America

10 9 8 7 6 5 4 3 2 1

CONTENTS

Acknowledgments   ix
Introduction
    The 10 most often asked questions
        about *Business Briefs*   1

1. POTENTIAL   3

    Action Plans   4
    Continuing Education   8
    Entrepreneurial Dreams   11
    Interviewing to Perfection   15
    Jumping Ship   18
    Networking Upward   20
    Résumé Magic   23
    Risk-Taking   26
    Salary Negotiation   27
    Shopping for an Employer   29
    Snagging a Mentor   32

2. PRODUCTIVITY   33

    Creativity Boosters   34
    Decision-Making 101   38
    Energy Enhancers   42
    Intuitive Edge   43
    Negotiating the Deal   45
    Paper Glut   49

Contents

Quiet Time   51
Reading List   52
Selling It   54
Smart Scheduling   55
Time Bandits   56

3. PERSONALITY   57

Projecting Confidence   58
Class Act   60
Cockiness Control   62
Gender Differences   63
Golf Anyone?   65
Interpersonal Communication   66
Obsequiousness   68
Personality Clashes   70
Signs of the Boring   71
Tooting Your Horn   73
Winning Attitude   74

4. PRESENTATION   75

Body Language   76
Lookin' Respectable   78
Memos that Sing   81
Review Time   82
Talking Tall—Part I   86
Talking Tall—Part II   89
Telephone Tact   95
Television Talent   97

5. PROTOCOL   99

Asking for a Raise   100

Business Cards 103
Business Etiquette 104
Communication Choices 106
Conflict Resolution 107
Dancing over the Boss's Head 108
E-mail Convention 109
Faxing Frugality 111
Foreign Customs 112
Lunch Manners 118
Office Presence 119
Power Seating 121

6. PRINCIPLE   122

Age Discrimination 123
Bigoted Bosses 124
Eco-Intelligence 125
Ethical Dilemmas 127
Office Romance 128
Personal Values 130
Race Relations 132
Sexism in the Office 134
Sharing Credit 135
Social Responsibility 136
Spotting Liars and Crooks 138

7. POWER   140

Acting Like a Leader 141
Brainstorming Basics 144
Delegation Do's and Don'ts 146
Fostering Teamwork 147
Hiring the Best 149

Contents

History's Lessons   153

Motivating the Troops   155

Power Vision   157

Project Management   159

Rewards and Incentives   162

Running the Meeting   164

Terminating with Tact   166

8. PEACE   168

Balancing Act   169

Callousness in the Workplace   171

Crush on the Boss   174

Doing What You Love   176

Dual Career Couples   177

Easing Career Jitters   179

Hating Work   180

Keeping Perspective   181

Kids-N-Careers   183

Loony Bosses   185

Mommy Tracking   187

Working at Home   189

Panel of Sharp Minds   191

ACKNOWLEDGMENTS

A standing ovation to the many experts who carved out time in their busy schedules to share their wisdom with me. Without that input, *Business Briefs* would be very brief, indeed.

Thanks, too, to three sharp minds who provided behind-the-scenes input: to my editor, Andrea Pedolsky; to my agent, Ellen Greene; and to my partner, Susan Ellis Wild.

Finally, a big hand to librarians everywhere—especially to those behind the reference desk at the Allentown Public Library.

INTRODUCTION

THE 10 MOST OFTEN ASKED QUESTIONS
ABOUT BUSINESS BRIEFS

So what's this book about?

It's about being successful, *really* successful, which means enjoying a chunky paycheck, yes. It also means liking yourself.

Is this a serious book or a funny book?

If the tone seems whimsical, that's only my response to having been forced to read so many shockingly dull management texts back in B-school days. The information contained in this book, however, is extremely serious and practical—coming directly from top experts around the world.

Who are these experts?

They're senior executives at big corporations (but no tobacco companies); successful entrepreneurs; well-respected consultants, speakers, and authors; professors at leading schools like Wharton; a couple of first-rate military minds (on leadership); Dave Barry (on creativity); and other authorities in their selected fields.

How'd you find all these people?

Some I'd hooked up with in the past, in the course of my own career, and while writing other books or magazine articles. Others I had read inspiring articles about in newspapers, magazines, or industry journals. A few I met through professional associations, university public affairs offices, and connections made on the Internet.

Introduction

Where'd the title come from?

Originally it was *Career Smarts*, but my editor suggested *Business Briefs*. I like it, because of its double meaning: Each entry is about business *and* it's brief. (No, nothing to do with underwear.)

How come it's "165 Guiding Principles" and not "164" or "166?"

Nothing magic about 165. I figured we could squeeze that many entries into a book this size. Worked out pretty well, actually.

How many phone calls did you make putting this book together?

Whew, let's see . . . I touched base with about 90 experts. Typically each contact involved two or three chats. That's, oh, about 225 calls. There were lots of faxes, e-mails, and FedEx packages, too.

Is there anyone you wanted to talk to, but couldn't?

Yes, Abe Lincoln. (See pg. 153.)

Is there anyone you talked to, but wish you hadn't?

Yes, Donald Trump's secretary.

Her: Mr. Trump would be more likely to talk with you if you had others in your book who were in his league.

Me: Er, Colin Powell isn't in his league?

Her: Well, have you talked to Bill Gates?

Me: Well, no.

Her: Fine, talk to Gates, then call back.

Why is the book divided up into 8 "P's"—Potential, Productivity, Personality, Presentation, Protocol, Principle, Power, and Peace?

Hey—it sounded cute. But, coincidentally, anything and everything I or anyone else could think about career success fit snugly into one of the category headings. Certain subjects probably could have gone under more than one category. If any choices seem arbitrary, they had to be. So sue me.

1·POTENTIAL

"Plastics," said the old family friend in the movie *The Graduate*—offering up the sum total of his career advice to the mixed-up young grad.

At the time (1967), that probably wasn't bad advice.

But perhaps we can do better. Perhaps *a lot* better.

This first section takes you headlong into the career world—giving you pointers on how to pick a good career (first, second, third, whatever), how to get into it with a bang, and how to know when the time has come to shift tracks—without getting barbecued on the third rail.

As you'll see, experts agree that a key to lasting success in today's career world is to be resilient, yet flexible—something like certain plastics.

ACTION PLANS

CUT A WIDE PATH

Yeah, the dusty old maxim holds some truth—aim for nothing and you're sure to achieve it. On the other hand, tomorrow's job market is as unpredictable as the wind. Aim for too narrow a job target, and by the time you get there, you may find opportunities have blown away. Look at all those bright young people who grunted through three years of law school only to then discover that the job market was choked with lawyers . . . One of those esquires might have been the "telemarketing professional" who interrupted your dinner last night.

> **"I often hear people say, 'I have to find myself.' What they really mean is, 'I have to make myself.'"**
>
> —Kent Nerburn,
> Letters to My Son

"You must have a strategy for career success, but it needs to be a flexible strategy, and you have to think very, very broadly in terms of career options," says Eugene Fram, professor of marketing at the University of Rochester. In other words, third-year students in law school need a few options between "lawyer" and "phone solicitor." And that holds true for the rest of us as well.

"The registrar at our college, who was college-trained as an accountant, is always joking 'Yeah, when I was six years old I dreamed of becoming a university registrar,'" says Fram. He points out that many of us could wind up in similarly unexpected positions—"If we keep our minds open, our contacts growing, and never stop looking out of the corners of our eyes."

INVEST IN YOURSELF

Some people put enormous time and effort into planning and preparing their winter vacations, flower gardens, and toddlers' birthday parties, yet they allow their careers to drift around like dandelion seeds—till they have fallen to the wet, moldy ground.

"The best way to reduce the chance that you'll ever find yourself unemployed is to position yourself in the business world. You need to think of yourself as a business entity and take total responsibility for planning, developing, and managing that entity," says Barbara Oldridge, a marketing and management consultant based in Bucks, England. "I came across an interesting and—to most people, I'm sure—unlikely role model for this the other day."

"I read an interview with Cindy Crawford in which she said that she thinks of herself as the president of a company that sells one product called Cindy Crawford. All of her decisions regarding that product—the work she accepts, the appearances she makes, the interviews she grants, and so on—are driven by marketing potential." That kind of outlook, says Oldridge, would ensure anyone career success.

Of course, a strategically placed mole can also help.

TAKE A PEEK AT THINGS TO COME

No one, not even Madame Rosa with her tea leaves and moustache can foretell the future. But there are some trends evident in the work world that offer pretty darn good hints as to where the job opportunities might be in five or ten years. Here, according to business futurist and management consultant Roger Herman, are a number of diverse trends. Keep them in mind when thinking about a career path:

- More people will be shopping from their homes using computers.
- More people will be working at home. Managers will be supervising people they've never met.

- Those who work in offices will find them more user-friendly, with better lighting, more open spaces, and workstations that are designed to be kinder on a person's muscles and bones.
- There will be many more day-care centers—both for young children and the soaring number of elderly.
- Space and undersea exploration will grow, a good part of it involving the search for minerals.
- As our seas succumb to pollution and overfishing, the growing of fish and crops underwater will certainly become a booming industry.
- More businesses—and bigger business—will be built on and around the Internet.
- Hospital-based health care will give way to home-based health care.

GET SUITED UP

Corporate life or a business of your own? You might start your career off the way Henry and Richard Bloch did in 1946, as two very young brothers with a common dream. In the Blochs' case, that dream eventually yielded one of America's largest and most successful companies—H & R Block. "But it doesn't always work out that way," warns Henry Bloch. "I'm the exception. We were in the right place at the right time—and we had a lot of lucky breaks."

"I wouldn't advise anyone else to go into business as I did," says the chairman of North America's largest tax preparation service. "I think a person should go out and get a job, get some experience first, and then perhaps think about starting a business."

Lori Rosenkopf, assistant professor of management at The Wharton School, agrees entirely. "Of course there are exceptions, but those who succeed in businesses of their own usually aren't starting from square one. I recommend that people begin new careers by working for established companies," she says. "It's a way to gain knowledge, make contacts, and have an opportunity to survey an industry for opportunities."

How long should you plan on spending in the corporate world before you even think of going out on your own? "There's no easy answer, although for most people five to ten years would provide a good base," says Rosenkopf. "A better guide would be to wait until such a time that you're getting interest from the outside world, people are starting to recognize your talents and expertise and begin to call you up with opportunities."

ACCEPT NO LIMITS

Yeah, it's entirely true that those who grow up amidst manicured lawns and attended the poshest private schools have an advantage. No question. "But even those born into the most disadvantaged homes and in the *poorest* communities can get where they want to go with enough determination," asserts Edward Donley, former chairman of industrial giant Air Products and Chemicals, Inc. and the creator of six not-for-profit corporations devoted to improving education in America. "Lincoln did it. Colin Powell did it. You can do it."

> **"Argue for your limitations, and sure enough, they're yours."**
> —Richard Bach,
> Illusions

"Education," says Donley, "is the vehicle that propels you along the road to success. If you didn't get the education you wanted earlier in life—then get it now. It's up to you. You can whine and complain about all the advantages you didn't have and set yourself humble goals. Or you can set your sights sky-high, roll up your sleeves, and crack open the books to get there."

CONTINUING EDUCATION

LOOK BEYOND THE CLASSROOM

Sure, to succeed in business you'll need some hard, textbook skills. But don't think that the road to success is paved only with pages from *Introduction to Accounting*. There are a lot of things to learn out there and a lot of places that offer learning opportunities. For example, creativity—the kind you'll need to come up with new products and marketing campaigns—is best learned by delving into a place where creativity is the primary objective, such as the world of the arts.

"Participating in the arts is enjoyable and can also be an investment in your career," says Roland J. Kushner, assistant professor of economics and business at Lafayette College in Easton, Pennsylvania.

"Movies can be great examples of creativity, and some, such as *Wall Street, The Player, Working Girl*, and *It's A Wonderful Life*, offer good insights into the working world," says Kushner. "Attending shows, concerts, art exhibits, and folk festivals can also be entertaining, yet valuable learning experiences."

VOLUNTEER AT WORK TO BOOST YOUR MARKETABILITY

What career skills will make you hot in the 21st-century and beyond? "They won't have a heck of a lot in common with the skills dad needed," says Wayne Brockbank, director of the strategic human resource planning executive program at the University of Michigan and consultant to such Fortune 500 companies as Dow Chemical, Texas Instruments, and Alcoa.

"Foremost, you will need flexibility," says Brockbank. "In a fast-paced environment the criteria for success can change quickly. You can't allow yourself or your department to be locked into a routine." *How to develop flexibility:* Volunteer to head a task force to analyze where the competition is going and how your company might respond.

Future managers must also be capable of developing people who can act on their own. "Rather than having eight subordinates, you may have forty. You must be an effective team leader," says Brockbank. *How to learn development skills:* Volunteer to work with two departments having conflicts with one another to effectively resolve the conflict.

The future manager will very much need to be self-aware, in touch with his or her own strengths and areas that need improvement. *How to become more self-aware:* Volunteer to solve a particular environmental problem by working with an activist group. "This type of problem is invariably a sticky one. You bet it'll test your mettle," says Brockbank.

"Tomorrow's corporate leaders will also need to be smooth talkers," says Dan Fogel, director of the executive education program at the Joseph M. Katz Graduate School of Business at the University of Pittsburgh. *How to become a better rapper:* Volunteer to talk on the rubber-chicken circuit—give as many presentations as you can.

IS AN MBA IN YOUR STARS?

The MBA isn't a bad thing to have these days, but is it worth your commitment of time and money?

First, not all MBAs are equal. In fact, there's a huge difference in average starting pay between the diamond-studded schools and the lesser-knowns. At Harvard, freshly minted MBAs are now greeting the corporate sunrise with average starting salaries of over $100,000. Even at highly respected, diamond-chip schools like the University of Texas or Indiana's Purdue, new MBAs are accepting more earth-bound salaries, averaging in the 50s to low 60s. At those cubic zirconia schools that would accept anyone who could pay, it's guaranteed that starting salaries are much, much lower.

Of course, years down the road, where you got your MBA, or even whether you have an MBA, won't be as important to prospective employers as your job performance. "By the time one is five years out, job performance counts almost exclusively," says Eric Greenberg, director of management studies at the American Management Association.

"So should you go for an MBA? It really depends," says Greenberg, mostly on what your long-range goals are. "In some careers, having an MBA—any MBA—is a necessity. In other careers, it doesn't matter." He suggests that rather than limiting yourself strictly to thinking about an MBA, you consider other advanced degrees. "The most sought-after managers these days are people with multiple specialties," he says. "In many cases, an advanced degree in engineering, information systems, or organizational psychology might be worth much more than an MBA."

SE HABLA OPPORTUNITY?

Lucky you. English is the international language of commerce. That means that you can usually squeak by just about anywhere without knowing a lick of Spanish, French, or Japanese. "Yet learning a second language opens doors—and arms," says Peter Blackford, director of the export division at Goodyear Tire & Rubber. "Working comfortably and effectively in a foreign country is going to happen a lot easier if you make an attempt to learn the language."

In fact, many companies won't even consider you for an international position—and even some domestic positions—without a second language.

Como aprender? "You can start with books and tapes and lessons, but the fastest way to learn is to sink yourself entirely into the other language— total immersion, to live with a foreign family and speak nothing but their language," says Blackford. If you can swing it, book yourself on a 10-day study-abroad program. You'll find them advertised in higher-brow magazines, such as *Harper's*, *The Nation*, and *World Press Review*.

ENTREPRENEURIAL DREAMS

ASK YOURSELF THE RIGHT QUESTIONS

The potential rewards of starting your own business are fantastic: big bucks, your own hours, own dress code, no boss gumming nasty Post-its to your chair. Of course, many entrepreneurial endeavors soon drown in a pool of high hopes, lost dreams, and sour creditors. It may, however, not be as rough out there as you think. "I've often heard this estimate of 90 percent of all small businesses failing within five years. I'm not sure where that comes from. According to the latest studies I've seen, the number is more like 40 percent. That's to say that about 60 percent—a good majority—of small businesses succeed," says Roland J. Kushner.

How to tell if you're likely to float or sink in the world of small business? "I'd ask you to make an honest assessment of your abilities in five areas," says Kushner:

- Can you handle many things at once?
- Are you self-disciplined?
- Do you have imagination?
- Are you willing to assume risks?
- Are you willing to initially invest all of your time?

GIVE REALITY THE TEST

It's become the mantra of the modern-day corporate executive: *If I lose my job, I'll become a consultant . . . I'll become a consultant . . . I'll become a consultant.* For some executives that's not a bad plan, but for others, they might as well be dreaming of becoming rock stars, Miss America, or the Pope—it just ain't gonna happen.

"A lot of people in the corporate world simply don't have the kind of skills that anyone outside of their particular companies is going to want. Others haven't the faintest idea how to sell themselves," says Eugene Fram.

How to know if you've got the stuff to make it as a consultant? "Get your feet wet," says Fram. "Do part-time consulting on evenings and weekends. You don't need to do much. Trying to land just an occasional job will give you a pretty good idea of your marketability." "And if you find out that consulting isn't in your stars," says Fram—"then it's time to start working on a better, more realistic 'Plan B.'"

DON'T BUY INTO STEREOTYPES

The successful entrepreneur works into the wee hours of the morning, eats meals on the run, spends New Year's Eve doing the books, and lives and dies for the business, right? Not exactly. "A lot of people think of the entrepreneur as a strange, processed kind of person," says Lori Rosenkopf. "But you don't have to have misplaced priorities, a dysfunctional personality, and a fanatical work ethic to be a thriving entrepreneur."

"In fact," says Rosenkopf, "that stereotype of entrepreneurs is nonsense. The creation of value through innovative products and services—the essence of entrepreneurship—can happen for any sort of person," she says. As Rosenkopf teaches MBA students in her course, "Innovation, Change, and Entrepreneurial Management," you can be a successful entrepreneur no matter who you are.

Rosenkopf asserts as well the radical belief that you can even be a successful entrepreneur without owning your own company! Within the right large corporate structure, she says, "a person may fulfill entrepreneurial ambitions by running a project or a department as if it were a company within a company. The professors at Wharton even have a term for it: *corporate entrepreneurship*."

EXPECT TOUGH TIMES AT THE DINNER TABLE

If you're resolute about going out on your own—and, please, don't do it unless you are resolute—be ready to ward off a lot of negativity from those around you. Family and friends are likely to get kind of edgy when you tell them that you're planning to give up a steady paycheck in favor of running your own business. Parents are often the worst—particularly if they've sunk thousands into a college education so that you could land a regular job.

"People around you will tell you you're making a stupid decision. I hear this from just about everyone who decides to take the entrepreneurial route," says Jane Applegate, whose syndicated column, *Succeeding in Small Business*, appears in dozens of newspapers nationwide. "You have to be prepared for that. And you have to have a thick skin and stand up to it!"

BEWARE OF SCAM ARTISTS

Want to get rich quick in a business of your own? Not work very hard? Put only a few bucks up front? It doesn't matter what your background or qualifications—we have a deal for you!

With corporate life getting meaner by the minute, many are looking for escape, and that escape is often in self-employment. In response, there's been a boom in scams designed to fleece wanna-be entrepreneurs. There are also the standard pseudo-scams, deals cooked up by owners of failing businesses looking to unload them on the first available chump.

How can you move into and operate your own business while side-stepping the muck? "Do your homework and you won't get burned," says Joseph Goldberg, director of the Bureau of Consumer Protection with the Office of the Attorney General of the Commonwealth of Pennsylvania. Here are your homework exercises:

Examine the books—and beyond. Some guy wants to sell you his business. He tells you it's a cash cow . . . customers rolling in the door

. . . cash flowing like wine. Fine. Let him prove it. "Look very carefully at the financial books," says Goldberg. And unless you are extremely adept at analyzing them, hire a lawyer or accountant to do so for you. And talk to others in the same business. Ask them if there are any ways in which revenues might be exaggerated or costs understated.

Think skeptically. "Any business that offers quick or unusual returns should always be suspect," says Goldberg. "So should any offer being made by someone who avoids answering reasonable questions."

Know who you're dealing with. The seller says, "I've been in business for eighteen years, successful, respected in the community." Truth or lie? Start with the local Better Business Bureau, the Chamber of Commerce, and the state attorney general's office. Talk to the seller's customers, suppliers, and employees. If you're dealing with a franchise operation, make sure you interview people who have previously bought into it. "Make sure you meet them face-to-face and actually see the operations," advises Holly Cherico, director of public relations and communications for the Council of Better Business Bureaus. "And talk to more than one or two—the first one may be the seller's brother-in-law."

INTERVIEWING TO PERFECTION

PAINT A PRETTY PICTURE

You got the interview. Yesssss! What now? "Being interviewed is an art—and there are a lot of bad artists out there," says Mark A. Case, director of the career development office at the Yale School of Management.

"The biggest knock-out factor in interviews is walking in with the idea that the resume will speak for itself, that you're there only to fill in any blanks," says Case. "Effective interviewing should include a well-designed presentation in which you differentiate yourself from other candidates, position yourself within the company, sell your unique package of qualifications." Here's how:

Differentiate yourself. "A lot of job candidates find it difficult to distinguish and separate themselves from teams they've been part of in the past," says Case. "You really need to talk about your special talents and achievements."

Play your position. Do your research. Get the full scoop on the company and the position for which you're interviewing. Make a list of the talents and skills that you'll need to get the job done in such a position. During your interview, show that you have those skills by giving specific examples. If you're applying for a position as a management consultant, for example, recount projects you've tackled in the past that show your intelligence, analytical skills, people skills, and ability to manage projects.

Sell yourself. "I can't tell you how many people in interviews say, 'I think I can make a big difference . . . ,' or 'I might . . . ,' or 'I would. . . .' Don't overuse qualifiers," says Case. "You want to say 'I am the right person for this job . . .' and 'I can make a big difference.' The distinction between making the assertion with the qualifier and making it without may seem minor, but the impact on the listener can be as different as night and day."

Sell yourself again. "Like any salesperson, you'll need to close the sale," says Case. At the end of your interview, ask whether you can have the opportunity to encapsulate. At that point, summarize your qualifications and how confident you are about taking the position. Thank the person for his or her time.

. . . And a third time. As soon as you get home send off a follow-up letter. "Start it off by again thanking the person for his or her time, and recapping important points discussed during the interview. Personalize your note—it shouldn't look like a form letter," says Case. Then make your final pitch—one more time, summarize your unique talents and how swimmingly you would fit into the organization and excel at the job.

EXUDE CONFIDENCE—NOT CONCEIT

The job interview is no time for modesty. "There's much too much competition not to be assertive and even bold," says Case. There can be, however, a rather fine line between "assertive and bold" and "conceited jerk." "The difference," says Case, "will often be expressed not so much in your choice of words, but in your body language and tone of voice."

Let's take two candidates, whom we'll call "Judy" and "Jennifer." Both women may make the very same pitch during their interviews: *In my last job I boosted sales by 30 percent, cut overhead by 20 percent, and was voted most valuable employee of the year.* But Judy says it in a way that is clearly intended to be for the interviewer's benefit . . . She sits up tall, bent slightly forward, looking directly into the interviewer's eyes. Her tone is one of enthusiasm and pride at sharing this information. She comes across as assertive. Jennifer, on the other hand, says it in a way that seems to be for herself. She leans back in her chair, legs crossed, eyes floating around the room. Her tone is one of ennui, a phony ennui. She comes across as cocky.

Judy will get the job.

DO THE DOLLAR DANCE

You spilled no soup on your lap at lunch, your palms and pits are still dry, and you're glibly chatting away—everything, in other words, is going perfectly. Then, all of a sudden, the air is stiller than death and your heart begins to go flub flub, for the interviewer has asked you the dreaded question: So, Mary Beth, what are your salary requirements?

This guy is no fool. He's trying to get you to show your cards before he shows his. What's running through his mind is "Mmmmm, this gal seems awfully eager, maybe I can get her for peanuts."

"Don't fall for his trap," says Sandra K. Allgeier, director of human resources for Providian Corporation, a financial services company based in Louisville, Kentucky. Instead, throw the question right back at the interviewer (sweetly, of course). Say something like . . . *Well, Douglas, I would like to look at the total picture, which would include future opportunities, base pay, and benefits. Could you give me some idea of your expected range of pay, as well as a sense of benefits and the chances for rapid advancement?*

If the joker still insists that you show your cards, give him a peek, but only that. Say something like: *Based on my research, I would expect a range in the area of, oh, $35,000 to $45,000. Is that consistent with your expectations?*

If asked for your current pay, you're stuck. Be truthful. "I know popular wisdom says to hold out on that information, but this really irritates employers and they eventually find out anyway," says Allgeier. Be certain to tell the interviewer if you are expecting a raise in the next three to six months, and how much that will likely be.

JUMPING SHIP

FIVE SIGNS THAT YOU'RE HOG-TIED

"**B**ob, there's something I've been meaning to discuss with you . . . I just wanted you to know that the odds of your getting a promotion around here in the next forty years are remote, at best. In fact, Bobby—" says the bossman, draping his arm around Bob's wilted shoulder, "I'd say the odds are far higher that NASA will discover that Saturn's rings are made of mango chutney."

Of course, in real life, Bob will never hear such a thing. Bosses are paid to get you to work hard, and you're not going to if you've been walloped with the morbid truth. If you're hog-tied to a dead-end position, you'll have to figure it out on your own. Here, according to business psychologist Michael W. Mercer, are the five signs to look out for—"any one of which could be a red flag."

1. Have you been in your job for over one and a half years with no concrete talk of promotion? "Most young fast-track employees get promoted every two years," says Mercer. "Anything less and you may be all dressed up with no place to go."

2. Has your boss been at his current job for three years or longer? If so, he's probably not going anywhere and neither are you.

3. Are your company, division, and department expanding? If the answer is no, no, no, then your chances for promotion are slim, slim, slim.

4. Have you asked your boss when you can expect a promotion? She should be able to give you *some* kind of time frame. However, if she evades your question or uses words such as *flattening, downsizing, reengineering, increased productivity, or streamlining*—you ain't goin' nowhere.

5. Do you fit into the corporate culture? "You can be the most productive, intelligent employee in the whole company, but you won't get ahead unless you get along with your boss, your boss's boss, and every other executive who could make or break your career," says Mercer. If these people duck into doorways when they see you coming, your head is already scraping the ceiling.

DON'T BE THE LAST TO GO

If your entire enterprise is going underwater, realize that the local job market will soon be awash in job applicants. "Obviously, this is one case where it pays to get a jump on the crowd," says Eugene Fram.

How early should you jump? There's no easy answer—and some individuals and jobs will always be more vulnerable than others. But if the company has been losing money for more than a year with no signs of a turnaround, if rumors are sailing that the company is about to be sold to out-of-towners, if a new management team has already been given control but doesn't seem to be taking hold, then it's probably time to start looking for a lifeboat.

NETWORKING UPWARD

PREPARE YOUR LIPS

Everyone appreciates the importance of the written résumé, and most job seekers will spare no expense to create a first-class product. Yet it's often not the written résumé that lands the great job. Rather, the key to success may be the short introductory telephone spiel you give to a prospective employer, or to someone who might introduce you to one.

"I really can't overstate the importance of having a well-honed, punchy presentation that concisely presents a clear and interesting summary of you. I call it the *verbal* résumé—and it is the essence of successful networking," says Clyde Lowstuter, cofounder of Robertson Lowstuter, a career development management firm based in Deerfield, Illinois.

Think of your verbal résumé as a radio spot designed to quickly gain a listener's attention. Just as your written résumé went through numerous drafts before its final, polished form, so it should be with the verbal résumé. "Revise it, refine it, practice it," says Lowstuter. "Read it into a tape recorder, say it in front of the mirror, rehearse it driving in your car." Then when you call to introduce yourself to someone important, your first utterance will be so remarkably articulate and thoughtful as to give you an instant air of authority and respectability.

TRY THE ELECTRONIC ROUTE

"Electronic communications (e-mail) can be an extremely powerful networking tool, both for making contacts in your company or outside," says Peter M. Saunders, director of the Rauch Center for Business Communications at Lehigh University in Bethlehem, Pennsylvania. "E-mail allows you to get to more people in important places than either the telephone or the written note."

"Although no one has yet to satisfactorily explain the strange phenomenon, many top execs today have their secretaries painstakingly filter all postal mail and phone calls, but those same execs will often read their e-mails themselves," says Saunders. "By taking advantage of this access, you can extend your network much faster and much further than you can with other modes of communication."

FIND THE AGENTS OF CHANGE

You've heard the adage before—get out of your office, meet people in other departments, extend yourself. Good advice, but let's face it, you've only got so much time and unless you're working in a hardware store or a luncheonette it's unlikely you can meet *everyone* in the shop. So where do you set your sites?

"If career advancement is among your priorities in life, you need to hone in on those people working to facilitate change," says Elaine Ré, popular speaker and trainer, and president of Ré Associates, a management consulting firm with offices in London, New York, and Albuquerque. "Align yourself with the agents of change in your company—introduce yourself to them, ask them lots of questions about their projects, and generally endear yourself to them," she says. "Then you'll be sitting pretty for a key position when their projects take off."

The way to find agents of change is through the corporate grapevine, says Ré. "Ask people, 'What's going on around here that's new and exciting and who's responsible for it?'" You can find agents of change in information systems, engineering, quality control—they "could be just about anywhere in the company," says Ré.

THINK BROADLY

Go to work for IBM or General Motors-type companies and you could easily spend your entire life networking only within your own

Potential

huge department and certainly within your own company. Don't. "The most successful people tend to have networks that extend beyond their own companies," says Lori Rosenkopf.

"It's actually dangerous to spend all your time networking within your organization," says Rosenkopf. "You wind up sharing the same sort of information, repeating it over and over. But by making contacts throughout the industry, or even in different industries, you expose yourself to varied kinds of information that you can potentially recombine to develop more interesting opportunities."

In other words, says Rosenkopf, "think broad, rather than deep." The best ways to meet people outside your organization?

- Professional societies
- Seminars
- Trade shows
- Trade associations
- Technical committees
- Online forums
- Charitable functions
- Community and church organizations
- Alumni gatherings

RÉSUMÉ MAGIC

MAKE IT SO ACTIVE IT WIGGLES

You've got a lot riding on that 8 x 11 sheet of paper you pop into the mail. Naturally, you want it to sing. To do that, "it's got to be a verb—one big, fat, continuous verb," says Mark A. Case.

"The biggest mistake people make on résumés is to design them to be descriptive, not active," says Case. "Effective résumés are not job descriptions." They must convey not your responsibilities on your last job—but your accomplishments, how they affected the bottom line, and by how much.

Descriptive (yawn): *Responsible for supervising staff of seven.*

Active (better!): *Reduced department overhead by 35 percent in two years by leading team of seven in streamlining the production process.*

Descriptive (blah): *Sold widgets.*

Active (more likely to land job): *Increased sales of widgets by 40 percent through innovative online marketing campaign.*

Other than your accomplishments, you should list a few personal interests at the bottom of the résumé—something to help break the ice when you go in for your interview. Think of hobbies (playing the piccolo), reading/movie interests (enjoy Stephen King), or volunteer activities (member of school board). Don't say anything so generic that it makes you sound like Will Whitebread ("Enjoy music" or "I like being physically fit"). And omit anything about religion, marital status, and children. "These are inappropriate," says Case.

CREATE A COVER LETTER THAT HELPS, NOT HINDERS

The typical résumé comes adorned with a cover letter. It goes something like this:

Dear Sir: [That's mistake #1]

Enclosed you will find my résumé. [Mistake #2] *I'm applying for the job as financial analyst. I have completed four years of business education at the University of Gotham, and I worked for two years in the accounting department at Joe's Hardware Emporium in Yonkers* [Mistake #3] *. . . blah, blah, blah . . .* [Mistake #4] *So you can see that I'm the quintessential candidate for the heretofore* [Mistake #5] *mentioned job of financial analyst.* [Mistake #6]

> *Sincerely,*
> Ain't Got A Chance

Explanations:

Mistake #1—Assuming testosterone. Are you certain that the person reading this letter isn't named Mary or Susan? (Unless you are certain, forget "Dear Sir" and "Dear Madam"). Go with "Ladies and Gentlemen," or simply "Good Morning," suggests Kay duPont, owner of The Communication Connection, an Atlanta-based consulting company specializing in helping leaders in business and government to become better communicators.

Mistake #2—Stating the painfully obvious. Isn't it self-evident to the person holding two sheets of paper that you've enclosed your résumé? "It's an insult and a waste of time to say so," says duPont.

Mistake #3—Repeating what's in the résumé. He (or she!) can also see clear as day that you have four years of business education at the University of Gotham—after all, you have it right at the top of your résumé.

Mistake #4—Chatter chatter chatter. Keep it short. "This person doesn't have time to waste," says duPont.

Mistake #5—Playing Chaucer. Er, look around. The Middle Ages are over. Don't use such old-fashioned pomposities as *heretofore, herewith, to wit, aforementioned, hereinafter,* or *pursuant to.* "Use only words that you use in everyday speech," says duPont.

Mistake #6—Lousy tailoring. "A cover letter," says duPont, "is a place to show that you've done your homework. Through your local library you can find out all kinds of information about the company. Do it. Use it. Your cover letter should reflect that you know the company and what it's about. Communicate that you don't want to be simply a financial analyst—you want to be a financial analyst for *this specific company*."

SCRUB YOUR COPY CLEAN

It seems unfair. You can pour *days* into preparing the classiest-looking résumé to be found anywhere between Wall Street and the Silicon Valley. You can spend hours in the books researching the company and write a cover letter that is insightful, witty, and wise. You can have all the credentials that the employer is looking for—and much more. But that employer will look at your material and within half a heartbeat, fling it disgustedly into the trash. Why? Because in the first sentence you misspelled a word.

"Bad spelling, grammar, and punctuation are *absolute killers* in the job market," says duPont. According to one survey, four out of five executives at America's largest corporations have declined to interview candidates *solely* because of an error found in a cover letter or résumé. Nearly two-thirds of those polled said that poor writing skills make a person seem like a dunce.

Don't be a dunce. Read and reread your material—and then have someone else you trust or two people you trust look it over. Don't put too much faith in your computer's spellcheck program! It will flag misspellings, sure. But it won't flag grammatical errors, or punctuation flaws, or entirely wrong words.

RISK-TAKING

DO IT WHILE YOU'RE YOUNG

For those readers born in the Space Age (circa 1960 and beyond)—listen up . . . Some special advice for you:

> **"Necessity is the mother of 'taking chances.'"**
>
> —Mark Twain

"By the time middle age starts rolling around, few of us are in a position to accept a lot of risk. We get in too deep with a nice style of living, a mortgage, and kids heading toward college," states Dennis P. Slevin, professor of business administration at the Joseph M. Katz Graduate School of Business at the University of Pittsburgh and a former CEO of four corporations. "I say if you're going to go west, young man (or woman), go when you're in your 20s or 30s and maybe you'll be running the ranch by the time you're in your 40s."

SALARY NEGOTIATION

TAKE IT STEP-BY-STEP

You have an offer pending. Decent job. After months of pounding out résumés your first notion is to jump like you've just found a scorpion in your Fruit of the Looms. Jump, however, and you'll live to regret it. At *no other time* in your relationship with that employer will you have as much power to negotiate. Use it.

Here are some pointers on post-offer salary negotiation from Sandra K. Allgeier.

Do your research. Find out what the market is paying—both low end and high end—for jobs like the one you are considering. Where on the scale are you, given your skills and experience?

Have your bottom line. Sometimes it is necessary to take less than optimal pay to gain the right experience. Other times it makes sense to hold out for the max. Do some intense personal assessment and determine what you want to make and how much you'll settle for—a rock-bottom figure. "You'll do much better in negotiation once you are certain of your own limits," says Allgeier.

Be patient. Don't ask about salary. Let them bring it up. Only exception: If you have strong beliefs that your pay expectations and what they can offer are light-years apart. In that case, say something like, "I am very interested in learning more about the position, but before we spend a great deal of time in discussion could you give me a sense of the pay range?"

Be cool. If you get an offer that isn't exactly going to put you on Easy Street, tell them that you will need to review the situation and get back to them. If asked if there is a problem with the offer, say that it is less than you were anticipating and that you need to think it through. "Don't let disappointment creep into your voice, stay positive and professional," says Allgeier. "If you have specific issues for which you can cite reasons for balking (I stand to lose $1,000 a year or more due to loss of profit sharing at my old job, etc.) state those—but not in an argumentative or whining fashion."

Go for what you can get. Having weighed the pros and cons, and deciding that you probably want the job, call back. Indicate that you'd like to discuss the offer again and come to an agreement. If you sense it is appropriate, ask if there has been any reconsideration of the salary offer. If the answer is no, ask if a hiring bonus is a possibility. Bonuses are often doable when the interviewer wants to hire, but the first year salary is limited by company guidelines.

SHOPPING FOR AN EMPLOYER

HOW TO PICK A COMPANY THAT'S ON THE RISE

You can have enormous business potential, but if you hitch on to a sinking ship your career isn't going anywhere but down. How can you assess a company before you move in the door? Do a "competitiveness audit" to predict the company's chances of surviving and thriving, suggests Dennis P. Slevin. Naturally, you want to examine the bottom line. But don't stop there. Look particularly close into four areas:

Does the company know where it's going? Does it have a clearly written mission statement? Is there a well-developed long-term business strategy? Has this strategy been clearly communicated to all levels of management?

Is there active new product development? Is innovation a priority at the company? Most importantly, look at how many new products they've come out with in the last few years and compare it to the leaders in the industry.

Where does quality rank? Is customer satisfaction a major goal of the company? Are customers involved in the product improvement process? Has the business established clear measures of customer satisfaction?

Do you get sweet vibes? Do people seem to take pride in their work? Does management seem to trust the workers? Do workers trust management? For rapid adaptation you have to have open communication and trust. Mean companies tend to lose out in the long run.

QUESTIONS FOR YOUR POTENTIAL NEW BOSS

Of course they're going to tell you that there's infinite opportunity for advancement—but how can you really know? "If I had only one thing to tell someone, it would be to ask your potential new boss for a history of his promotions," says Michael W. Mercer. "Fast-track bosses always pull their star employees along with them. If your boss is moving up fast and furiously, then you're likely going to ride along right under his wing."

Another business expert, a publishing executive who says she's worked for several vile and brutish bosses, recommends another must question to ask during an interview: "You know that part where you're asked whether you have any hobbies or outside interests? If the person interviewing you will be your future boss, I would definitely suggest flinging the question (diplomatically and nonchalantly) right back across the desk," she says. "If you get nothing but yammering about how hard he works (in other words, he has no hobbies or outside interests), you'll know that this person is a workaholic, and he's likely going to make your life miserable—as most workaholic bosses do."

> **"The pay is good and I can walk to work."**
>
> —John F. Kennedy
>
> (on becoming president)

DON'T SIGN ON WITHOUT MAKING THE ROUNDS

The glossy, full-color recruiting brochure paints a picture of a progressive, dynamic, sensitive place to work. "Fun, creative atmosphere," it says on page one. On page two there are pictures of happy, smiling people. By page three, geez, you're ready to pay them for the privilege of working there. But can recruitment brochures and promises made by interviewers be relied on to give you a true feel for the place? "No. There's often a lot of hype," says Mark A. Case.

"The latest thing in recruitment brochures is to showcase diversity—they'll feature one or two African Americans and Asians, and maybe a Hispanic, smiling as they do their work. But be careful," says Case. "If you're looking for happy diversity, make sure you talk to enough people in the company to know whether it really does exist."

"Talking to people—other than those two or three interviewing you—is essential for getting the scoop on a number of important things," says Case. "Talk to as many people as you can who work there. If you can, find alums from your school who will often be very straightforward with you." "Here," says Case, "is the information you should be trying to ferret out in these talks."

What are the company's work values? "So many companies are now emphasizing having a life—that is always something to be wary of," says Case. "Some corporate cultures—despite what recruiters tell prospective employees—promote being in the office all the time."

How kicked-back is the atmosphere? The way people dress, whether they call each other by first name, and how the offices are decorated are all telling signs of a company's culture—and whether or not you'll fit in. Be careful though—certain companies, particularly in the computer and entertainment fields, can deceptively appear very laid-back and casual because people wear jeans. In reality, this casualness may be covering up an extremely tense working environment.

What are the company's ethical values? If a company has a history of noncompliance with the law—polluting the environment, discriminating against women and minorities, conducting misleading marketing campaigns, you can bet you won't find mention of this in the recruitment brochures. The way to find out is to check with the Chamber of Commerce, the Better Business Bureau, local environmental groups, and the town newspaper.

SNAGGING A MENTOR

STOP LOOKING IN ALL THE WRONG PLACES

It helps—often a lot—to have someone who can take you by the hand, teach you the ins of the business, advise you on career direction, and give you brutally honest feedback on your performance. True mentors are tough to find—but not as tough as you may think. The problem many people have is that often their top candidate—or only candidate—for mentor is the very person on the entire planet least suited for the job.

> **"Always try to rub up against money, for if you rub up against money long enough, some of it may rub off on you."**
>
> —*Damon Runyon*

"It can't be your boss. You want your boss to assume that you know what you're doing—even if you don't. The boss is the one person in the whole universe you don't ever want to see you naked," says Robert Teufel, president of Rodale Press, Inc.

Better candidates? "A good mentor doesn't have to be much older and wiser than you," says Teufel. "In fact, I wouldn't go for anyone too much beyond your level of experience—that person is likely to be out of touch." Rather, says Teufel, "look to someone who's achieved something in another company. It could be a person you know from industry connections or even a neighbor or friend in a whole different industry.

"I've had a friend for thirty-five years who has been really useful to me in my career," says Teufel. "He was CEO of a pharmaceutical company. Whenever we talk he brings a whole different set of experience and skills to the table."

2·PRODUCTIVITY

L et's turn to such matters as creativity, decision making, intuition, negotiating skills, and organizational abilities. These are the tools of productivity: They determine at the end of each day whether you have anything to show for your labors, other than eraser shavings on your pants legs and a few empty coffee cups.

Like other tools, these need occasional sharpening, oiling, and sometimes a complete overhaul. You shouldn't assume that because you got an A in your freshman creative writing class that your creativity couldn't use a boost. Or that because you had no problem this morning deciding which cereal to eat that your decision-making powers can't be improved.

We've assembled here a diversified panel of experts, including several of the sharpest minds in business, a U.S. Air Force general, a New York State Supreme Court judge, and America's best-known humor writer, Dave Barry. If these guys can't give your productivity a lift, no one can.

CREATIVITY BOOSTERS

ROLL OUT THE ASSOCIATIONS

Looking to slap a hot name on your company's latest product? Wondering how to get the creative juices flowing? "The secret to strong creativity is thinking by association," says Marsh Fisher, cofounder of Century 21 Real Estate, now the head of IdeaFisher Systems, Inc., a California-based computer software company.

> **"Imagination is more important than knowledge."**
>
> —Albert Einstein

Association works by starting with a particular word or concept and then coming up with as many related terms as you can. They may be synonymous terms, or opposites, or related to each other in any way whatsoever. So, let's say we're trying to come up with a name for a new wrinkle cream . . .

What word do we associate with wrinkles? Old. What word do we associate with old? Young. What do we associate with young? Health . . . fitness . . . springtime. What do we associate with springtime? Birds . . . flowers . . . sunshine. And so on. As you make these associations, keep a written list. The longer the list, the better. "Wear yourself out developing options—your mission is to accomplish total 'braindump,'" says Fisher.

After you've finished your first list, begin another. Perhaps start with the word cream. Repeat the process. Then make another list. This time, start with the word smooth. From these multiple lists rearrange the words in as many ways as possible. "That," says Fisher, "is where you'll find your new idea, your solution, your new product name."

THINK THE UNTHINKABLE

Long before there were computers, televisions, automobiles, or even bicycles there was Leonardo da Vinci drawing up designs for flying machines. And decades before any machine would ever fly, there was Jules Verne telling stories of people traveling by rocket to the moon. "Such creative thinking is possible only when one is willing to think the unthinkable," says Andre Alkiewicz, founder and managing partner of Perception International, a corporate consulting firm specializing in the early identification of worldly changes.

"The handicap of most people who wish to be creative is that they rely on what they see as an obvious item or subject and then try to derive from it a new creation," says Alkiewicz. The problem with that kind of creativity—let's call it derivative creativity—is that any improvements you make will likely be only incremental. If even that. Windows 95 comes to mind. Or *Rocky II* to V.

> **"No one can possibly achieve any real and lasting success or 'get rich' in business by being a conformist."**
>
> —*J. Paul Getty*

"The way to achieve Leonardo-type creativity is to start from scratch," says Alkiewicz. Suppose you're looking to develop a new car. You could start with your basic four-door Chevrolet, and then try to figure out what would make it better. Or, you could do what Leonardo might have done . . . Think wildly: Who says cars have to have wheels? . . . Or doors? . . . Or run on gasoline or electric power? Maybe they could hover? . . . Maybe they could be propelled by magnetic force? . . .

"Those who can think the unthinkable will always come up with the most creative solutions and the greatest breakthroughs—and then they'll inevitably be followed by hordes of incremental 'me-too' guys," says Alkiewicz.

FIVE TIPS FROM ZANY DAVE

Dave Barry, nationally syndicated humor columnist and author, says that on rare occasions he'll experience a flash of inspiration that will lead him to his keyboard where he'll slam out something screamingly funny. "Much more often," he says, "the creative process is a slow, frequently tedious one. I'll spend a lot of time with an idea, putting it down on paper, diddling with it, and moving things around."

So that you don't diddle with your ideas in vain, here are a few suggestions from Barry on getting the most out of your creativity:

Go wild. "Don't worry about what others think of your ideas," Barry says. "People limit themselves a whole lot because they're so afraid that someone somewhere is going to make fun of them."

Find your peak hours. "I think we all have a time when we're most creative," says Barry. "For me, an hour in the morning is worth three hours at night."

Get comfortable. "I always write with my feet up on the desk, keyboard in my lap," says Barry. "That's what works for me."

Let ideas simmer. "Ideas often need to cook," says Barry. "I'll often break from my writing to pick at my guitar, sometimes pick at my teeth, anything to pass a little time."

Don't force it. Sometimes when picking his guitar and his teeth isn't enough, Barry will put an idea aside until the next day. "It's amazing how much easier things can be the next morning," he says.

DEVELOP YOUR IMAGINARY BRAIN TRUST

The meeting gets started with George Washington suggesting that the competition be hit hard. Ben Franklin jots down a few notes with his quill pen. Ernest Hemingway says something about having to take the bull by the horns. And Salvador Dali sips espresso and twirls his mustache.

It could be the beginning of a great brainstorming session.

"When I need to think creatively, I'll often visualize myself sitting around a table with people I find larger than life. I imagine, for instance, that I'm surrounded by George Washington, Ben Franklin, and Salvador Dali," says Virginia Littlejohn, CEO of The STAR Group, an international marketing and consulting firm. "These people become my brain trust—and assist me with my creative decision making."

In order to learn more about her "helpers," their thought processes, and how they might suggest running a business, Littlejohn says that she reads lots and lots of biographies. She'll then choose her imaginary brain trust based on her needs of the day. "Some days Ben Franklin and George Washington may be of most help; other days it might be Picasso or even Rube Goldberg."

"The process of setting up an imaginary brain trust," says Littlejohn, "allows you to get out of your own ruts and habits. It's an extremely effective creativity tool."

DECISION-MAKING 101

TAKE IT STEP-BY-STEP

Solid white shirt or striped blue? Coffee or tea? Sports section or comics? It starts first thing every morning—the continual process of decision making that we call life as a functioning adult. When we get to the office, the process escalates: Which project gets your priority? What phone calls get returned first? To whom do you offer that new contract? You could argue that sharp decision making is to job and career success what hopping is to a kangaroo—you aren't going anywhere without it. Yet so few of us ever get any training.

> **"It is a capital mistake to theorize before one has data. Insensibly one begins to twist facts to suit theories, instead of theories to suit facts."**
>
> —*Sherlock Holmes*
>
> A Scandal in Bohemia

Below, a quick course in rational decision making from a guy who makes big decisions for a living, Gerald S. Held, a justice of the Supreme Court of the State of New York.

Ask yourself how important is a decision you're making. Are you making a decision that could make or break a multimillion-dollar deal? Or are you choosing a vendor to keep you supplied in paper clips? Ask yourself, "How many minutes, hours, or days does this decision deserve?" advises Justice Held.

Don't shoot from the hip, unless you have to. Your next step is to ask yourself how much time you have to make this decision. "Is there a train bearing down the tracks or not?" asks Justice Held. "Some problems need immediate solutions, others can wait."

Get as much input as you can. Given your time frame for making this decision, endeavor to collect as much information as possible. At this stage, says Justice Held, "it's better to listen than to talk." And he suggests talking to people in the know and people of different walks of life. "Try to get a good cross-section of opinions—the more the better."

Aim for consistency. You don't want to be rigid, says Justice Held. On the other hand, it's extremely important to let others know that you're not wishy-washy, either. Consider decisions you've made in the past involving similar circumstances. Review your decision back then, and ask yourself if it makes any sense to reverse yourself now. Do so only if you have a compelling reason.

Be prepared to justify your decision. "I'm all in favor of explaining decisions, especially if you're turning someone down or putting someone in a humble position," says Justice Held. "It helps lay the groundwork for future good relations."

SIDESTEP THE BOOBY TRAPS

People make bad decisions for all kinds of reasons. Among the managerial set, perhaps the biggest pitfall is short-term thinking. "Almost every day we see business managers issuing some new policy without giving any thought whatsoever to the long-term ramifications," says Keith Weigelt, associate professor of management at The Wharton School.

Not far behind short-term thinking comes cockiness. "Most of us are way too overconfident in our decision making," says Weigelt. He recommends that whenever you're sitting on an important decision, ask yourself first how the current environment could change and how that might affect your call. Then force yourself to imagine all the things that could possibly go wrong if you decide to do such and such.

"Look for bad news," says Weigelt. "If you can, find someone else who will tell you the bad news. Too many people make a decision then look only for confirming information to bolster their decisions."

RELIEVE PERFORMANCE ANXIETY

It's a classic catch-22. To make the best decisions, you should be cool and collected. But few people in the business world today walk around in anything close to that state of mind. Then a decision comes along needing to be made quickly. And that, of course, only infuses more stress into your already frazzled soul.

"The corporate landscape is littered with bad decisions made from overreaction to situations based on stressful emotions," says Bruce Cryer, executive director of corporate programs at the Institute of HeartMath, a California-based think tank whose mission is to develop scientifically-based tools to improve decision making, productivity, and overall health.

"The key to making the best decisions is to break out of the catch-22, to find a way to at least temporarily achieve a neutral, rational state of mind," says Cryer. Now it would be just dandy if every time you had to make a decision, you could take a stroll in the sand, unfortunately, you probably can't afford such a time-consuming luxury. You can, however, *mentally* walk on that beach. And you should.

One of the institute's core techniques is called Freeze-Frame. "First," says Cryer, "recognize your stress, then stop whatever you're doing, concentrate on your heartbeat for 10 seconds or so, and follow up with that "walk" along the Maui shore. Or go swimming with the swans in the cool pond behind your grandparents' house. Or remember the fun of playing with your kids. Try to recall an experience that left you with a sense of wonder or appreciation about life," says Cryer. If you need help jogging your memory, glance at those family photos up on your bulletin board.

"Once you're feeling more balanced," says Cryer—"and it should only take about a minute—you'll be in the best position of your life to make decisions. Then, and only then, can you step back and make full use of your intellect and intuition—without wild emotions fouling up the process. Once the decision is made, pat yourself on the back and appreciate all the time and energy (and money) saved by making a good decision instead of a bad one."

STAND BY YOUR CALL

"There comes a time when a decision has to be made and put behind you so that you can move on to the next thing—even if some people are left unhappy with your decision," says Gerald S. Held.

If malcontents are persistent in wanting to change your mind, you may have to let them know, gently but firmly, that the matter is a done deal, says Justice Held—"What I'll often say to these people is that I may be wrong, but I'm *definitely* wrong."

DON'T BEAT YOURSELF UP OVER THE BAD ONES

It's okay to look back over decisions you've made in the past. "But only so that you can learn for the future—*not* to beat yourself up for having made bad decisions," says Marvin C. Patton, major general, United States Air Force (ret.) and successful entrepreneur.

"Everyone who makes decisions will sometimes make bad ones," says General Patton. "You've got to just say to yourself, 'Well, that's a bummer—I'll do better next time.' You can't let it eat you. You can't let it defeat you."

> **"Failure is the condiment that gives success its flavor."**
> —Truman Capote

ENERGY ENHANCERS

GIVE YOURSELF A QUICK KICK START

A lot of things can leave you feeling like overcooked linguine, particularly on midweek afternoons. It may be poor sleep, a lousy diet, lack of exercise, depression, or the flu. If fatigue hits you particularly hard, or is an everyday occurrence, see your doctor. Most occasional slumps, however, are a result of boredom and stress and can often be tackled with a few simple countermeasures.

"You'll need to experiment to find out what works best for you. Not every person will find the same things energizing," says Marcia Yudkin, consultant, seminar leader, and publisher of *The Creative Glow*, a newsletter for enhancing work productivity. Below, some 5-minute energy boosters that Yudkin says some people have found extremely effective:

- Go outside and look at the sky
- Browse through travel magazines
- Take a brisk walk
- Stretch
- Swap jokes with someone
- Tinker with a broken machine
- Knit
- Work on a crossword puzzle
- Listen to music
- Watch tropical fish
- Shoot a ball into the trash can
- Meditate
- Call a friend for a chat

INTUITIVE EDGE

TRUST THAT GUT FEELING

That *aha!* sensation called intuition is nothing short of "the most important management tool there is," says Virginia Littlejohn. She is one of a number of business luminaries who say that intuition's position as "second fiddle" to quantitative analysis has severely wounded American industry.

"Far too much business in the United States has been dominated by the 'quants' (quantitative, analytical thinkers). That's not what's needed to take us where we need to go at this time," Littlejohn says.

The intuitive process is "almost visceral . . . I use my entire body as a decision-making instrument," says Littlejohn. "When I find the right answer, I get a surge of what feels like electricity, a flash of ecstasy, a total eureka! reaction."

> **"It is only with the heart that one can see rightly; what is essential is invisible to the eye."**
> —*Antoine de Saint-Exupéry,*
> The Little Prince

"There's a huge difference," says Littlejohn, "between productive intuition and acting on wild hunches. Acting on a wild hunch is running out and buying a stock because Joe Bologna, the bartender, said it was a hot one. It's spending $100 in lottery tickets with the number 77 in them simply because you woke up that morning feeling that that was the thing to do."

On the other hand, productive intuition is a process of reaching down inside of you and fishing out information that is already there.

Productivity

Obviously, you need to make sure the information gets there—"I marinate myself in information, bombard myself with news, different ideas, perceptions, facts . . . any information I can get hold of," says Littlejohn.

"Once you've done your homework and have a bank of knowledge from which to draw, the key to getting it out in a useful form is to get yourself into a deeply relaxed state," says Littlejohn. When she's trying to intuit a solution, Littlejohn likes to use a variety of deep-breathing exercises and relaxation techniques. She also favors relaxing music, the best of which, she says, "are the baroque big hits of the 1700s, especially those of Mozart."

NEGOTIATING THE DEAL

DON'T WALK IN COLD

Richard Nixon may have had his faults, but the man was, without question, a first-rate international negotiator. What made him so? "He could do what expert negotiators have to do—he was able to see the world from the opposition's vantage point," says Dennis P. Slevin, professor of business administration at the Joseph M. Katz Graduate School of Business at the University of Pittsburgh and the former CEO of four corporations.

"As a first step to walking into any negotiation you need to learn as much as you can about the person or organization you're negotiating with," says Slevin. "Based on what you believe are his goals, try to anticipate the moves of your opponent, and plan your possible responses." If you have someone to role-play with, go through a few dress rehearsals.

"The better planned you are," says Slevin, "the more likely you are to succeed." Nixon often did.

HAVE A SOLID PLAN

Good negotiators don't wing it. They know in advance what they'll offer, what they'll accept, and at what point the guy on the other side of the table will get to see them wiggle out of the room. Good negotiators also know better than to focus on only one issue—they realize it is critical to be able to have things to trade off.

Expert negotiator Elaine Ré, popular speaker, trainer, and president of Ré Associates, a New York-based management consulting firm, says that the best preparation for walking into any negotiation is to have a plan, which clearly lays out (for your eyes only) your issues and your negotiating goals.

As part of this plan, you need to determine your "maximally favorable (but supportable) position," says Ré. "You don't really expect to get this, but it's a starting point for the negotiation." Basically, it's as low/high as you can go without coming across as a lunatic—you can at least make a halfway reasonable argument why you should get this deal. You should also have penciled down what you're really asking for and expect to get if all goes right. You should also figure out what your least favorable, but still acceptable position would be—as well as your breaking point.

Ré suggests that you prepare a matrix for yourself using the following outline. Note: The number of issues may well exceed three.

	Issue 1	Issue 2	Issue 3
Maximally Favorable (but Supportable) Position:			
Really Asking For:			
Least Favorable, but Still Acceptable Position:			
The Deal Breaker:			

Source: Negotiation Matrix is a Copyright © 1991 Ré Associates Inc., 101 W. 12th St., New York, N.Y., 10011. All rights reserved.

KNOW THE TRICKS OF THE TRADE

Call 'em ploys. Tactics. Tricks. You can choose to use them or you can choose not to. But you darned well better be aware of them—because sooner or later someone is going to use them on you. Here, according to Elaine Ré, are perhaps the three most common ploys made in business negotiations:

1. **Good guy/bad guy.** You take a tough, even unreasonable stance while your partner portrays himself as friendly and sensible. After hearing your outrageous demands, your partner's requests will sound so incredibly reasonable that they are likely to be accepted. "This is the ploy most often used because it is so effective and so hard to detect," says Ré. "The other person will never be sure it's a ploy." *How to deflect (if used against you):* If you suspect that two clowns are pulling this number on you, throw it right back at them. Say, "Look, you two talk it over and work it out between you. Then come back and we'll chat. I want everybody to be happy with this deal."

2. **Authority limits.** You'd just love to make the deal, but, sadly, the person who must give final approval isn't available. This puts you in a pretty position. The joker across the table is stuck with whatever deal he gives you, but you, sly fox that you are, get to come back at any time and renegotiate—simply because your "boss" or "members of the board" didn't like the deal.

   How to deflect: Whenever possible, try to negotiate with the person who has full authority. Perhaps you are negotiating with that person but you're being told otherwise—then, says Ré, "it's time to invent a higher authority of your own." That way, at least, the four of you (you, the one you're negotiating with, and your two higher authorities) are all on equal ground.

3. **The bogey tactic.** You say, "I really love your product and it's undoubtedly worth every penny you're asking, but my funds are limited, and I can't possibly go over $1,000, or whatever. This can be a sweet tactic because it sidesteps defensive justification and ugly haggling. On the other hand, if your offer isn't taken you'll wind up eating crow to get the deal.

   How to deflect: Tough. You're almost in a take-it or leave-it situation. Have a firm handle on what you're own bottom line is, and don't cross under it. Stroll away if you need to.

SHOW THOSE PEARLY WHITES

Regardless of any strategies or tactics you employ when you get to the negotiating table—and regardless of any that are used on you—airing contempt or hostility is never going to help your cause. "A smile and harmony are the two most powerful negotiating tools I know of," says Osamu Yamada, general manager of WKKJ, a Japanese branch of a Hong Kong-based manufacturer of electronics equipment. "We all prefer to do business with people we like."

PAPER GLUT

HAVE NO MERCY

"Paper flow accounts for the lion's share of all corporate activity today—and an ever higher percentage of employees' wasted time," says Jeff Davidson, management consultant, professional speaker, and popular author. The only way to keep from being eaten alive by paper, says Davidson, "is to ruthlessly regard each piece of paper that enters your personal kingdom as a potential mutineer, rebel, or disloyal subject."

"Every piece of paper has to earn its keep and remain worthy of your retention," says Davidson. "Were it to speak it should be able to immediately convey its value to you. And if it can't convey—send it flying right into the recycling bin."

GET DECISIVE

Call it the Scarlet O'Hara (I'll think about it tomorrow) Syndrome. Call it the Executive Shell Game. Call it the potentially largest waste of time and energy in the Western world. We're talking about the shuffling of papers back and forth, from one side of the desk to the other, from in-box to windowsill to the floor and back to the in-box again. We're talking about the procrastination of paperwork that has undoubtedly sunk many a career, many a company.

What to do?

"There are only four things that should be done with every piece of paper you encounter," says Stephanie Winston, president of The Organizing Principle, a time-management consulting firm, and author of *The Organized Executive*.

Productivity

- Throw it away
- Refer it to someone else (delegating responsibility)
- Act on it
- File it in a proper place for future retrieval

If you choose the last option, Winston suggests clearly marking a toss-out date on top of the file folder—if it isn't used by that date, it's history.

"The same principle," says Winston, "should also apply for e-mail notes and voice mail messages."

QUIET TIME

YOU'VE GOT TO MAKE IT FOR YOURSELF

It's doubtful that Einstein developed his theory of relativity in the midst of constant interruptions. "Some projects simply will need your undivided attention," says Dennis P. Slevin.

How, in today's world, do you get to give anything your undivided attention? You do it by allotting yourself some quiet time—say an hour or two a day in which you escape entirely from ringing phones, chatty colleagues, knocks on the door, and obnoxious beepers. How do you get quiet time?

- **Announce it to the world.** Put a note on your door. Have your secretary stand guard. Let your voice mail tell people to leave a message or call back.
- **Duck and hide.** If you live near the office, run home for an hour or two. Or find a quiet spot in a local diner, public library, or park.
- **Juggle your schedule.** Come in early and enjoy the silence before the start of the business day. Or come in late, and get your quiet time after the shop has closed.

READING LIST

HOT PICKS

To maximize productivity you need to keep up on the world around you. Reading is essential. But there's so much to read—and so little time. What should you be reading to advance your company and your career? What's a waste of time? A poll of the experts yielded a few suggestions. Go out of your way to read:

Periodicals

The *Wall Street Journal* (Cited by many experts—"And don't just read the business columns," says one communications executive. "Good leaders step outside of the narrow focus on business and become truly educated people. Read the middle column of the first page; it's always about something interesting and new.")

Business Week ("I'm always amazed how much I learn from each issue," says one manufacturing VP.)

Inc. magazine ("Offers stories about things that have worked for small businesses and things that haven't," says one successful entrepreneur.)

Harvard Business Review ("Quite often an article on something I'm dealing with at the moment," says a company president.)

Harper's and *Utne Reader* ("You'll need something left-of-center to lend balance to the rabidly right-wing opinions expressed on the editorial pages of the *Wall Street Journal*," says one Washington public relations exec.)

Books

Good management texts—For ideas, see "Panel of Sharp Minds," starting on page 191. Many of the best of this genre were authored by experts interviewed for this book. Also:

Truman, an autobiography of Harry S. by David McCullough. ("A fascinating account of the life and career of a man with extraordinary leadership qualities," says one B-school professor.)

Mutual Aid by Petr Kropotkin. Rather than seeing evolution as a process of competition and "survival of the fittest" (as Darwin has been paraphrased), Kropotkin shows that cooperation is what ultimately determines the success of both species and cultures. "And what Kropotkin wrote certainly extends to business cultures," says Alec Sharp, an information systems consultant, educator, and speaker with Damex Consulting Group, Ltd., based in West Vancouver, British Columbia. "In business I've seen countless examples where cooperation was better for all concerned."

Don't waste time with junk mail or articles and books promoting silly fads ("I've read many; never got a valuable bit of advice out of any of them," says one CEO.)

SELLING IT

DO IT WITH YOUR EARS

No matter what your career choice, there will be, at some point, selling involved. You may be selling a product, a service, an idea, or yourself. A gadzillion books and articles will tell you how to sell, but there's one common cord that runs through all of them: In order to sell something to someone you first have to know what that someone needs.

"The most successful salespeople are those who can see from others' perspectives. You always want to speak in terms of the interests of the person you wish to sell," says Stuart Levine, CEO of Long Island-based Dale Carnegie & Associates, Inc., the popular people-skills training organization. How do you know what those interests are? "You need to ask lots of questions," says Levine, "and listen very carefully to the responses."

SMART SCHEDULING

KEEP SHARP LISTS

If you're smart and well-organized you'll keep a list of all the things you need to get done. If you're real smart, you'll keep two lists," says Stephanie Winston.

One list (which can be in a spiral notebook or, if you're into high tech, a handheld organizer) should be a compendium of everything you need to get done, both in the short- and long-term: Initiate a new project, hire an accountant, pick up your dry cleaning, write a novel, whatever. A second list should then be prepared on a daily basis, picking out only those, say, five to ten projects that you need to do next.

> **"Next week there can't be any crises. My schedule is already full."**
> —Henry Kissinger

Your next step, says Winston, "is to rate those more immediate projects in terms of importance and urgency." The top two or three projects might rate a 1. The others will be your 2s and 3s. After you've rated them turn to your day's calendar. "Carve out a special period, perhaps an hour or hour and a half to deal with the 1s," says Winston. "The 2s and 3s can then be done during your downtime," she says, "like the 15 minutes between morning meetings or the 20 minutes after lunch but before your 1:30 teleconference."

TIME BANDITS

TAKE INTERRUPTIONS IN STRIDE

There are a number of ways to deal with people who interrupt you when you're trying hard to work. For instance, you can strangle them. Most management experts, however, prefer a more subtle approach, like telling your uninvited guest that you'd love to chat but you're 10 minutes late for a meeting with the Pope. Or, an even subtler, yet perfectly workable technique is to stand up, move toward the door (merely suggesting you have an important meeting with the Pope), and then turn back to your desk after the sucker gets the hint and leaves.

Yet another approach is to try and change your mind-set—to think differently about interruptions. "Try to view them as opportunities," suggests Stephanie Winston. "As long as your priorities are getting done, interruptions may not be so bad—especially if you can look at each one as an opportunity to advance your own projects and agenda."

3·PERSONALITY

Nine out of ten bosses (more or less) say that their most trusted and valued employees stand out not for their Ivy League diplomas and not for their stunning way with facts and figures—but for their attitudes, charisma, and smoothness in the social arena.

We're talking personality here.

Discussed in this section are such matters as temperament, sensitivity, communications style, and the ability to butter over conflicts. If you're not already the kind of person that others want to spend time with—and do business with—the advice presented here may just give your sagging career the face-lift it needs.

PROJECTING CONFIDENCE

YES—YOU CAN FAKE IT

In talks with the Guys Up Top, competence and confidence are given the Corporate Olympic medals for respect-winners. But by the time you're in your late 20s, a few years into the job, a certain level of competence starts to get taken for granted. That's when confidence grabs the gold. "What I look for in a young person in a management position is someone who carries himself well, dresses properly, and above all has an air about him of self-assuredness," says one petroleum industry executive.

Maybe you already have self-assuredness because mom and dad told you that you were a wunderkind. Or maybe you have confidence because your boss has gushed so much about your work that you can't help but have confidence. But face it, if you're like most young people starting off in a career you think of yourself as basically a weenie with ears. So how does an eared weenie exude confidence? *By faking it.*

"A lot of people have the extreme misconception that in order to act a certain way (like confident), you first have to feel it. But research shows that if you act confident, you'll *feel* confident," says Michael W. Mercer, a business psychologist with The Mercer Group in Barrington, Illinois. "By acting confident, even if you're not, you'll not only gain respect on the job," he asserts, "but you'll also improve your emotional health."

NO ONE IS PERFECT—NOT EVEN YOU

During your morning affirmations you look yourself in the mirror and say, "I'm good! I'm *real* good! I'm the best damned thing since

Post-its!" You get to work feeling pumped, but that's when you're told that you blew last week's presentation and the juiciest contract in history went to your competitor. What's left of your charred soul sinks slowly into your chair, you proceed to wallow through the morning, writhe through the afternoon, and make it home feeling as mighty and confident as a boneless chicken.

If your confidence is on a roller coaster, it's time to reach for more level ground. "You have to be willing to make mistakes because they're going to happen. You can't let it crush you every time you've tripped up on something," says Marvin C. Patton. "The only guy who never made a mistake is the guy who never tried. Especially if you're going to deal with big issues—you have to accept that on occasion there will be big mistakes."

CLASS ACT

SHOW A LITTLE CARE

Some people have class. Others don't. Those who do have class tend to fare a lot better in life. What is class? It means tucking in your shirt, using utensils at the table, not belching in public, and all those other things that mom tried to get you to do long ago. But that's only the start. "Here's how people display class (or lack of class) in the workplace," says Thomas Horton, former chairman of the American Management Association:

> "Everyone has an invisible sign hanging from his neck saying, 'Make me feel important!' Never forget this message when working with people."
>
> —Mary Kay Ash

- *People with class* do whatever it takes to make others feel at ease. "Two guys, Joe and Jim, go out on a business dinner, and Joe drinks from the finger bowl, mistaking it for a clear soup. Jim sees this, and so that his colleague doesn't feel like an idiot, he drinks from his finger bowl, too. That's class," says Horton.
- *People with no class* are sarcastic, nasty, domineering, and rude. They make others feel hot under the collar.
- *People with class* don't draw attention to themselves. They wear clothes that are neat, clean, and never too loud or revealing.
- *People with no class* wear high skirts, low-cut blouses, or outfits that overwise scream "lookee here!"
- *People with class* remember others' names.
- *People with no class* say, "Heeeey, yo, yeah, hey, how's it going, dude?"

- *People with class* decorate their offices tastefully: a plant here or there, maybe a small picture or two of the spouse and kids, a painting on the wall.
- *People with no class* turn their offices into shrines of self-adoration, packed with things such as softball trophies, poster-size blowups of the lucky bride or groom, or a mural-sized picture of themselves shaking hands with the mayor.

COCKINESS CONTROL

HONESTY WILL KEEP YOU EARTHBOUND

Yeah, maybe all the world's a stage, but that doesn't mean you have to win an Oscar. Strut your stuff, sure. Act confident, absolutely. But lay it on too thick and you may come across as arrogant. And *that*—acting like an Eddie Haskell in pinstripes—is how many young execs eventually turn silk tie up.

> **"If I only had a little humility, I'd be perfect."**
>
> —*Ted Turner*

"I think a lot of younger people tend to think that the only way to compete is to prove that they know more than their older colleagues. It's this 'I'm great; I'm the greatest-thing-since-sliced-bread' attitude that often gets them in trouble," says John Clizbe, senior partner with Nordli, Wilson Associates, a group of management and consulting psychologists based in Westborough, Massachusetts, and New Haven, Connecticut.

According to Clizbe, the key to achieving balance between self-confidence and arrogance is in realizing your own shortcomings—and openly acknowledging them. "The 28-year-old who says, 'I really don't know how to do this or that,' or 'maybe there's some part of this problem I've never dealt with before,' actually leads them to project more strength," says Clizbe. "I think that owning up to where you aren't strong is a part of self-confidence."

GENDER DIFFERENCES

BOTH SIDES NEED TO BEND

Any two people can have a spat. But dissension between men and women in the workplace often takes on a particular flavor. "There are certain personality traits and modes of communication that tend to differ between men and women, and these differences often make it difficult for the two camps to achieve harmony," says Carol Rudman, a Long Island-based management development trainer who works with companies such as Motorola, AT&T, and American Express.

Rudman, who authored *Frames of Reference: How Men and Women Can Overcome Communication Barriers—and Increase Their Effectiveness at Work*, says that the following three areas are often the most ripe for cross-gender misunderstandings:

1. **Directions and criticism.** Men, particularly when in supervisory roles, tend to be rather direct. When overseeing a project, a man might say to a colleague, "Do it this way, not that way." Women tend to be more subtle, less direct. A woman supervisor in the same role might say, "You ought to perhaps think about doing it this way." Because of these incongruous styles, a woman getting directions or criticism from a man often winds up feeling picked on and worthless; the man getting criticism from a woman often winds up feeling confused.

   Making peace: Men need to exercise more tact around women; women need to be more direct with men.

2. **Interruptions.** Men tend to break into conversations more frequently—and they tend to not take offense when someone does it to them. "Very often when one man interrupts, another man will interrupt right back—it's all good humored, and it can be very

productive," says Rudman. On the other hand, women generally prefer to take turns talking.

Making peace: Women should learn to interrupt right back when a man interrupts; men should learn to read the signs that they may be hogging a conversation.

3. **Emotions.** Men are trained not to express their emotions and are therefore often misread by women (as well as other men) as not having emotions. Women, who receive no such training, tend to express emotions more freely and may be seen by men as moody and unstable.

Making peace: Women need to realize that men do feel pain, fright, and happiness; men need to realize that women who express their emotions can nonetheless be just as competent and rational as any guy.

GOLF ANYONE?

MASTER THE SUBTLE ART OF MIRRORING

To gain respect in the business world you don't need to be a Leo Buscaglia hug-everyone-and-everything-including-the-Xerox-machine kind of person. "On the other hand, your handshake and smile are essential respect-builders," says Michael W. Mercer.

"A good chunk of commanding respect is getting someone to like you," says Mercer. "They (the guys in charge) are more likely to give career opportunities to those they feel most comfortable around." Ah, but how can you get someone to like you who is old enough to be your dad, drives a Buick, drinks manhattans, and enjoys elevator music? "The answer—as impossible as it sounds—is to find common ground," says Mercer. Like the country-club politician who rolls up his sleeves when addressing a group of Teamsters, you must learn the art of *mirroring*."

"Mirroring," explains Mercer, "means subtly changing your style so that you seem similar to the people you are with." Obviously, if your boss wears a fine worsted wool suit and you wear a Fine Young Cannibals T-shirt, you're not mirroring, you're rebelling. If you want her to respect you, suit up. More realistically, if she leans toward you, lean toward her. If she speaks quickly, speak quickly. If she speaks slowly, speak slowly. If she orders a manhattan—at least try one. "People crave to be around people who seem similar to themselves," says Mercer.

But wait. Must you—should you—prostitute yourself by becoming something you are not? "Not at all," says Mercer. "People who get along easier with other people naturally act a little differently with each person they're with," he says. Example: Would you tell exactly the same joke to your mother that you would to your buddies? The key to mirroring is "acting a little like . . ." while still maintaining your individuality.

INTERPERSONAL COMMUNICATION

NEVER TOO LATE TO LEARN

In school you learned that the Nile runs north. That sentences shouldn't start with "And." And that Thomas Jefferson chopped down the cherry tree. Or was it George Washington? Critical as this kind of information is to your business career, it would have been nice if you had also picked up a little formal education on communicating with other people. But you probably didn't.

Yet experts say that knowing how to relate interpersonally could be the single biggest factor in determining one's success in the world—even more than intelligence or fancy suits. Here are a few things that every adult should know, but many—far too many—don't.

Don't cut others off. "Helping" others to end their sentences is rarely appreciated. It's not a sign that you are brainy or psychic; it's a sign that you're rude. "Don't do it," says Aviva Diamond, president of Blue Streak/A Communications Company, a Los Angeles-based firm offering training in media and relationship skills to corporate executives.

Examine your interactions. Communication often gets muddled because we really don't know what we want to say to another person. "But every situation has an unwritten agenda," says Diamond. "Stop and ask yourself what you want to get out of your interactions with people." Are you trying to relay information to them? Get information from them? Express your feelings?

Critique, never crush. This world is full of varied opinions, different ways of doing things, and diverse values. That's what makes life so much fun. Occasionally someone will drive you nuts. "It's okay to criticize and disagree, but make sure that no matter what the content of the discussion, your tone still shows respect and caring for the other person," says Diamond.

Get feedback. Most of us can't really hear ourselves speak. As a result, most abrasive people often don't realize that they're abrasive. Ask family and friends what your tone of voice conveys. Don't have any friends? You have your answer.

Respect boundaries. In any business environment, no matter how stuffy, it is always appropriate to act human, to show caring for others. That includes exchanging birthday cards, showing heartfelt congratulations for such things as promotions and childbirths, and asking how the Caribbean vacation went. But, says Diamond, "a place of work is not a forum in which to discuss such things as marital problems, religious convictions, or anything else of a deeply personal nature."

OBSEQUIOUSNESS

CAN THE APPLAUSE AND CHUCKLES

All right, if the truth be told, we've all done it. It's hard to be in the presence of The One Who Signs The Paychecks and not exude at least a little canine devotion . . . "Hey, Bob. Nice tie! (Wag. Wag.) Saaay, how's that ab-so-lu-te-ly brilliant kid of yours?"

"Obsequiousness is almost an instinctive thing," says Denis Boyles, coauthor of *The Modern Man's Guide to Life: Advice and Information About Everything*. "It's really something you need to watch out for." Why fight your natural bent to express eternal allegiance and uncompromised regard for the mighty and influential? Because, unless the boss is a complete moron or egotistical lunatic, he'll know exactly what you're doing—and he won't exactly respect you for it. "As much as bosses want agreeable employees, they also want people they can trust," says Boyles.

Robert Teufel, president of Rodale Press, Inc., agrees. "I've had the experience of being given credit in front of a large audience for an idea that was allegedly mine—although the idea was only in small part mine," recounts Teufel. "Hearing that praise didn't make me feel especially good, nor particularly warm about the person giving the credit."

Excessive flattery, as experienced by Teufel, however, may not even be the most common or egregious act of obsequiousness in the corporate world. "The number one bootlicking crime is over-amusement. It's *amazing* the amount of inappropriate corporate laughter that goes on—people laughing at the boss's stupid jokes or even things that aren't meant to be funny," says Stanley Bing (a pen name), *Forbes* magazine columnist, author of *Crazy Bosses: Spotting Them, Serving Them, Surviving Them*, and a senior executive at a large corporation that he insists remain nameless.

Bing's rule: "If you find yourself laughing loudly in the boss's presence more than once every two or three weeks, that's probably a sign that you're exceeding the general level of acceptable bootlicking."

RATION THE PRAISE

Not *all* compliments to the boss qualify as obsequiousness. "All people—even bosses—have some good points. To speak of things that the insecure and overextended executive does well is an act of humanity—not just an act of bootlicking," says Stanley Bing.

What if you honestly think your boss does a lot of things well—should you pile on the praise and risk being seen as the consummate bootlicker? "You need to be aware of your boss's level of discomfort," says Bing. "Shifting of feet, darting of eyes over your shoulder or around the room, these are signs that the boss thinks you're being a weasel."

PERSONALITY CLASHES

WHAT EXACTLY ISN'T CLICKING?

Beth hates Nancy. John can't stand Ed. Deb cringes whenever in the same room with Kyle. Sound like your workplace? Personality conflicts are inevitable, and emotions can run particularly high in a pressurized environment like many of today's offices. What to do when feathers get ruffled? Here are some tips from Alan Weiss, founder and president of Summit Consulting Group, Inc., in Greenwich, Rhode Island:

> **"Love your enemies, for they tell you your faults."**
>
> *—Ben Franklin*

Don't get sucked into acrimony. If someone is being rude to you, being rude right back isn't going to help matters much. Instead, consider asking—in as nonhostile a voice as possible—"Why are you so angry?"

Focus on observable behavior. If a particular someone is always showing up late to your meetings, it's okay to confront her by asking, "Why are you always late to my meetings?" What's going to be counterproductive is to start pointing out what you think are her many character flaws. . . . "You're so inconsiderate. . . . You're so self-centered. . . ."

Narrow the field. If someone is continually acting like a heel around you, there's likely some unresolved issue between you. Ferret it out. Talk to them and find out where you differ. It's much easier to deal with specific topics than the fuzzier concept of a "personality clash."

SIGNS OF THE BORING

ARE YOU A WALKING AUTOBIOGRAPHY?

Many a career has been throttled not because a person is incompetent or lazy, unintelligent or crass, but simply boring. You know the type . . . Stands alone at company functions, sipping Snapple iced tea, trying to make eye contact with the multitude who circle about, everyone fearful to tread too near. If he happens to glom onto you, he'll typically launch into something tedious, speaking slowly, describing in painful detail something or someone from his distant past.

> **"The secret of being a bore is to tell everything."**
>
> —*Voltaire*

What can you do to make sure you're never the pariah of the party?

"Most boring people just talk about themselves. At the end of each day I replay every conversation I've had. I ask myself whether there was a good exchange, or whether all I did was talk about myself," says Stuart Levine, CEO of Long Island-based Dale Carnegie & Associates, Inc., the popular people-skills training company. As scintillating as you think your life is to others, you should have other things to talk about. "Make sure you're constantly reading and learning about new and exciting things," says Levine. "And most important, make sure you listen, as well as talk."

DON'T BE A RAMBLER

Do other people frequently cut you off in mid-sentence? Do their eyes glaze over in your presence? If you answered yes to both questions, chances are good that you are a rambler, a person who doesn't know when to stop talking, a person who can't complete a single thought without taking detours onto other subjects, like the time when George O'Brien visited his brother, Michael, in Buffalo and his neighbor, Sam, got his finger caught in the car door and how tragic that was but George took him to the hospital because his four-wheel drive, which is red, is so good in snow and the roads are so often snowy in Buffalo in January and . . .

STOP!

> **"A healthy male adult consumes each year one and a half times his own weight in other people's patience."**
>
> —John Updike

Being a rambler is not going to win you friends, and it certainly isn't going to help your career. "But you can learn to control it," says Aviva Diamond, president of Blue Streak/A Communications Company, a Los Angeles-based firm offering training in media and relationship skills to corporate executives.

Step #1: Realize you're rambling. (Go back to those two questions asked above.)

Step #2: Before you even start talking, figure out what you want to say. Ask yourself what it is that the other person needs to hear. Then get to your point as quickly as possible—cutting out all the peripheral junk.

Step #3: Shut up.

"The heart of business communication is dialogue—not *monologue*," says Diamond. "You are playing a Ping-Pong game. That means you hit the ball and then someone gets to return it."

TOOTING YOUR HORN

DON'T HIDE IN CORNERS

No, you don't want to be the office bag of wind. But neither do you want to go about your work too inconspicuously, asserts Robert Tusler, a consultant specializing in project risk management, based in Surrey, England.

"I was employed in a big computer center when I learned this lesson," says Tusler. "I had been working 14 hours a day making certain that all went smoothly—it came from being a merchant seaman where one had a fix-it culture. When my annual appraisal came around, my manager said 'You haven't done anything this year.'"

Gulp.

"After that I made certain to make my usefulness known," says Tusler. "When I saw a potential problem I decided first how I would fix it, and then I'd let it land squarely on the boss's desk before walking in and saying, 'No problem, Ray. I can sort this out for you in ten minutes.' This was when my career began to really move ahead more effectively!"

Many years later, working as an independent, Tusler maintains a similar philosophy. "The same concept applies in consulting. If the client does not know that you have fixed his problem, he will resent the money he is paying you!"

WINNING ATTITUDE

CATCH WHAT YOU SAY TO YOURSELF

Those little dialogues we have inside our heads can and do affect our attitude, which, in turn, greatly affect our performance.

Annmarie Hanlon, president of AHA Business Consultants, a group of corporate marketing advisers based in Lichfield, Staffordshire, England, suggests banning the word "problem" from your vocabulary. "It is negative and helps no one," she says. "Replace it with 'challenge,' 'situation,' or 'issue'—and then deal with it."

"I also recommend seriously monitoring the use of the word 'can't,'" says Hanlon. "It is often nothing but an excuse for 'would prefer not to.'"

DON'T BE AFRAID TO THUMP

Can you self-inject yourself with enthusiasm? You bet. What would football be like if the players didn't whoop it up, banging themselves on the helmets and whatnot before the big play? Prior to your next big play, you might try a little whooping yourself.

"Before making an important phone call, get yourself hyped up," says Ian Traynor, senior partner with Traynor, Kitching & Associates, a consulting firm based in York, England, that specializes in strategic marketing. "Smile. Laugh. Wave your arms around. Thump the table. Whatever it takes to get yourself really fired-up and cooking."

And what of your colleagues' reactions to your telling enthusiasm? "Forget it," says Traynor. "Either your coworkers will understand because they do it themselves, or they won't." In the latter case, don't worry about it, he says, "because your career is going places that they can't even imagine."

4·PRESENTATION

o you, like, um, you know, have like a hard time getting the right words out when you speak in public? Do your memos wind up as thick and stuffy as the original draft of the *Magna Carta*? Do you have a tough time figuring out what to do with your hands when you're chatting with the boss? Or which shoes to wear with a blue suit? If you answered yes to any of these questions, read on.

In this section we consult with some very sharp executives and topflight consultants on the subject of presentation—be it live, on the phone, or in the written word; be it before an audience of one or one thousand. As a bonus, you'll find invaluable tips on how to present oneself in that stickiest and most fidgety of corporate settings—the annual review.

Read what the experts say. Practice your rap. With luck, you'll never need to clarify yourself, as did former Michigan governer George Romney, when he told reporters—"I didn't say that I didn't say it. I said that I didn't say that I said it. I want to make that very clear."

BODY LANGUAGE

STAND AND BE COUNTED

Your posture and walk say a great deal about you. Slumped shoulders and a shuffle tell the world that you lack confidence and vitality, and given any new project or job, you'll likely blow it. On the other hand, standing erect and walking lively sends out greater signals of success than wearing a custom-made suit.

"You should stand as if you have a vertical string running through your body," says Gloria F. Boileau, a California-based communications and image expert whose clients include Rolls Royce, Westinghouse, and the Internal Revenue Service.

And what to do with those hands while you're standing around looking so sharp? Many people move them into the "fig leaf," crossed in front of one's private parts; others move into the "reverse fig leaf," with hands to the rear. Everyone from time to time digs those hands deep into the pants pockets, as if looking for cookie crumbs.

All three of those positions communicate "I'm uncomfortable," says Boileau. Better solution? "If you want people to see you as confident and relaxed—" she says, "then keep your arms and hands ready at your sides, lifting them when appropriate to help you punctuate your speech."

GLOW AT POWWOWS

Most people see meetings as nothing but a tremendous waste of time. That's not true. Whether or not any work ever gets done, meetings provide unique opportunities for people who rarely meet to check each other out—and make judgments about each other's talents and potential. If you want to look like a smart cookie, someone deserving of responsibility, raises, and promotions, then listen to Ian Traynor, senior partner with Traynor, Kitching & Associates, a consulting firm based in York, England:

"At meetings, don't sit back in your chair. Sit upright, but try to get relaxed," he says. "Lean forward slightly to make an important point. Look at people (but don't stare) when they are talking—and actively listen to everything they are saying. You want to give the impression that you find whoever is speaking to be the most important, scintillating person on Earth," says Traynor, "even if that person is something less than coherent."

LOOKIN' RESPECTABLE

THE ABC'S OF BUSINESS ATTIRE—FOR HIM

If you run your own locksmith or convenience store, you can pretty much dress as you like. But as soon as you enter the Big Corporate Landscape there are certain rules. If you don't go by them your bosses or clients may think you don't know them—and that may get them to wondering what else you don't know. Below are a few tips on dressing for respect from G. Bruce Boyer, image consultant and author of numerous fashion books, including *Eminently Suitable: The Elements of Style in Business Attire.*

Picking a suit. Simple choice of colors: navy blue or mid to dark gray. Look for quality, but don't shoot a month's salary. "It's good politics not to dress better than your boss," says Boyer. The most important criteria is fit. A well-fitted jacket is crease-free. (If too small, you'll see horizontal creases. If too large, you'll see vertical creases.) The shoulders shouldn't extend out more than 1/2 inch beyond your shoulders. The sleeves should hang straight from the shoulder to the elbow to the cuff. The jacket should be long enough to cover the line where your buttocks meet the back of your thighs.

Putting on pants. Well-fitted trousers will just touch your shoes. At the waist, they should be worn midway between the hipbone and your bottom rib. "Most men wear trousers too low," says Boyer.

Adding the shirt. Your shirt and suit need to work as a team. The sleeves of your shirt should hang from 1/4 to 1/2 inch below the jacket cuffs. The collar should ride 1/2 inch above the jacket.

Making an outfit. Neckties are where corporate men can be expressive. Take your pick of stripes, paisleys, dots, or even sailboats—just make sure you aren't too expressive. The safest, albeit dullest, combo is to wear a plain suit, plain shirt, and plain tie. But the better alternative is to mix in a pattern or two—although not the same pattern twice. For instance, you can wear a pinstriped suit, a solid white shirt, and a solid red tie. Or, you can wear a plain suit, a thin-striped shirt, and a paisley tie. But don't wear a striped shirt with a striped tie, unless the stripes are significantly different (such as pinstripes on the shirt and wider diagonal stripes on the tie).

Shoes. Plain black, with laces. Well-shined.

Haircut. Clip out pictures from magazines or newspapers read by businessmen (the ads from the *Wall Street Journal* are good). Pick a head you like, show it to your barber, and tell him, "this is what I want." If you're balding, keep your hair extra short. Do not take long strands of hair from one side of your head and string them over your dome—you'll look like a guy foolishly trying to hide his balding. Even worse is a cheap toupee.

Miscellaneous. "Accessories have an importance that outweighs people's realizations of them," says Boyer. "I recognized this a few years ago after my sister bought me a Mont Blanc pen—everybody noticed it right away." In addition to a classy pen, carry a good leather briefcase and a fine calfskin wallet. Do not wear any jewelry other than a simple wedding band (if you're married) and a quality watch with an unadorned face. ("You can do without the barometric pressure in Moscow," says Boyer. "And scuba watches should only be worn by divers.") College or other lumpy rings with colored stones won't earn you respect anywhere outside of a barroom brawl.

THE ABC'S OF BUSINESS ATTIRE—FOR HER

There's a world of difference between men and women, but it shouldn't be expressed in the workplace. "The same basic rules that apply for men also apply for women, although women decidedly have more latitude," says Boyer. Here are a few quidelines to follow:

Presentation

Suiting up. You can't go wrong with gray or blue. In all but the most conservative corporate cultures, taupe, a laid-back mauve, or flat terra cotta would also be perfectly acceptable. The more exuberant colors, such as orange, emerald, or hot pink, should be saved for weekend wear. The fit of the jacket is extremely important. For women in particular, it's crucial that the fit around the chest not be too tight. Make certain that the lapels don't flare out when the jacket is buttoned.

Putting on skirts. Skirts should be worn slim but never tight. There are three acceptable lengths: at the knee, an inch or so below the knee, and an inch or so above the knee. That's it.

Neckwear. Don't wear a necktie. Go with a blouse with a simple collar, a bow, or a scarf.

Making an outfit. Match solids with patterns. Or match patterns—but make sure that any two patterns you wear are of different scales. So, if your scarf features broad stripes, combine it with a jacket that has fine stripes. If your shirt has small dots, don't wear a bow with dots, unless the dots are very large.

Shoes. Plain pumps only. They can be black, or they can match the color of your outfit. Women are lucky here. "A guy doesn't get to wear blue shoes," says Boyer.

Stockings. Go with the color of your skin or a shade or two lighter or darker. No vibrant colors. No patterns.

Jewelry. Keep it simple. Avoid long, dangling things that make a racket when you move. Also avoid anything that's going to reflect the light. "You don't wan't to send out beams in the middle of a meeting, forcing colleagues to shield their eyes," says Boyer.

MEMOS THAT SING

USE TIGHT WORDS

There's an epidemic in the corporate world. Not long after young employees join a large organization, they catch this horrible disease that causes them to use big, bureaucratic-sounding words when simple words would work just as well—much better, in fact.

"Never use a large word if a small one will work," says Kay duPont, owner of The Communication Connection, an Atlanta-based consulting company that helps leaders in business and government become better communicators. To write memos that are as smooth as Velveeta, as readable as traffic signs, as unpretentious as white socks, refer to the following "Corporatese"/English dictionary, courtesy of duPont:

Corporate Jargon	Plain English
Originate	Start
Minimize	Reduce
In conjunction with	And
Substantial	Much
Endeavor	Try
Utilize	Use
Initiate	Start
Facility	Office
Requirement	Need
Contingent upon	Depends on
Facilitate	Lead
Alternative	Choice
Modification	Change
Incorporate	Blend
Obtain	Get

REVIEW TIME

COVER YOUR ASSETS

The degree to which you razzle-dazzle the boss during a 50-minute closed-door conversation will never be as important as how you razzle-dazzle him—with your work—throughout the year. But the first thing to remember before your next review is that your boss can't possibly *recall* every coup you've pulled off over the past twelve months.

"Who's going to be first in line for the money? The person who does the best job of reminding the boss how good he or she is," says Mike Deblieux, a human resource consultant in Tustin, California. "We tend to remember those things we do well, and we assume that others do too—but the fact is, bosses *don't* remember," he says. "If I'm your boss, keeping track of ten people, I've got ten people's sets of accomplishments to remember—by review time they all get muddled together."

The way you present your accomplishments during a review may be as important as the accomplishments themselves. Your presentation needs to be concise, specific, and—to the greatest extent possible—closely related to the company's bottom line. In other words, says Michael W. Mercer, a business psychologist with the Mercer Group in Barrington, Illinois, "What typically makes the greatest impression is showing how you measurably increased revenues or decreased costs—everything else is fluff."

In the field of banking, explosive numbers at the end of the year are what drives careers. "The results are in the figures," says Ken Daley, senior vice president/division executive with Chase Manhattan Bank. "At review time I want to know what an employee did to affect net revenue." In the case of a loan officer under Daley's command, "the bottom line equates to finding new clients and keeping—and growing—old ones."

But what if you're in a field—like human resources or marketing—where it's tough to show how you directly affected revenues? In that case, says Daley, "show me how you helped someone who directly pulls in revenue." In other words, show how indirectly you upped the bottom line.

TURN NEGATIVES INTO POSITIVES

"Anyone from time to time can have a bum year. But that doesn't mean you have to have a bum review," says Peter Blackford, director of the export division at Goodyear Tire & Rubber in Akron, Ohio. "Obviously, an employee who exceeds expectations is going to be in good standing at the end of the year. But clearly there are times when failure to do so is beyond someone's control," he says. "In that case, the way the employee handles the failure will be of utmost importance."

> **"The only completely consistent people are the dead."**
>
> —Aldous Huxley

For instance, imagine yourself a few years ago accepting the Yugoslavia account for Goodyear. It's hard to sell tires when mortar fire has flattened your market. But rather than looking shot and wounded at review time, says Blackford, "tell me how you made the best of a bad situation." For instance, "explain to me how you had hoped to do $10 million in business but half the country was inaccessible, so you concentrated your efforts on a few major accounts where you could still do business. And even though you only did $5 million, you managed to increase market share . . ."

Mark Cipollini, top manager of 61 Pottery Barn stores nationwide, says that for a store or district manager to make good in the retail business, two things matter most—sales figures and payroll control. The laws of the retail universe; however, dictate that not every year can be a banner year. "Sluggish times call for snappy action plans," says Cipollini—and a good time to present one is review time.

"The way to present figures to me during a poor sales period is to do so in the form of an action plan," says Cipollini. "Express your understanding of what happened and why—with an emphasis on what you're going to do about it." If employee turnover was too high, for instance, "tell me how you're going to recruit new people and follow up with training."

Ken Daley says that the worst thing to do if you've had a bad year is to gun through a review blasting others. "You've got to be honest," he says, "show me you understand why it was a bad year, and tell me how you're going to turn it around. Tell me what you've learned. Those who can admit to mistakes move way up the list for promotion," he says.

SMASH THE CEILING

A promotion, of course, is the Nobel Prize of the review process—or at least it should be, if more money is your goal. "It's a myth that people can earn lots more money in their present positions," says Mike Deblieux, a human resource consultant in Tustin, California. Most raises without a concurrent promotion will barely hike your paycheck enough to buy yourself a Matchbox Mercedes—forget the real thing. "The way to bankable raises," says Deblieux, "is by depositing yourself into a new job code—and a new pay scale."

What's important to remember around review time, says Michael W. Mercer, "is that there are two kinds of promotions." There are real promotions, and then there are promotions made to justify a pay raise. An example of the latter might be a promotion from "Account Supervisor" to "Account Manager." The responsibilities don't change, at least not much, but the title looks more regal.

The "pseudopromotion," says Mercer, is but one way you can work with your boss to reach glimmering career heights. Remember, even if he thinks you're the greatest hire since Fermi joined the Manhattan

Project, the system often limits him in terms of how much he can boost your salary—at least in your present position. That's where you and your champion might pull together as a team. The personnel policy says your salary can't slide up more than 3 percent in your present job? Show your boss how much you've earned for the company and ask him if he can give you a pseudopromotion, if not a real one.

The boss says she can't promote you? There are other ways to get ahead, says Mercer—"the key is to be flexible." How about a onetime $2,000 bonus in compensation for your hard labors? If a bonus isn't possible, how about an extra week's vacation? Or maybe a car phone at company expense? "One bargaining chip that's hardly ever used are convention trips," says Mercer. "When I worked in a corporation, I'd get my boss to send me to at least two conventions a year in spots like Florida during the winter," he says. "Then, I'd take a few days off after the convention and enjoy a nice vacation. You'll never know what you can get—unless you ask for it," says Mercer.

THINK A YEAR AHEAD

"Shortly after your review for 1996 is a perfect time to talk with your boss about your hopes and goals for 1997," says Michael W. Mercer. "You need to ask specifically what you need to do in the next year to get a 1 or 2 rating or a promotion next time around—and don't accept vague answers." While the boss talks, take notes. You'll use them a year later to make your big leap.

One advertising account exec calls this process "wedging them in." Says the 32-year-old Washingtonian, "You need to pin them down and get it in writing—so next year there's no dispute."

Pull this off suavely and the boss is unlikely to notice that he's been "wedged in." Ken Daley says, "It's O.K. to get a contract with the boss." In fact, he adds, "once you've asked the boss exactly what you need to do to get promoted, the next step might be to push for a reevaluation in six months rather than waiting for an entire year to pass."

TALKING TALL—PART I

STAGE YOUR OWN DRESS REHEARSALS

Actors rehearse. So do athletes, ministers, and rock stars. Yet many businesspeople seem to think they can perform in public without ever having practiced. Right.

"I don't know a single politician who doesn't rehearse," says Leslie A. Dach, former Dukakis campaign communication director. "But many execs think they're too busy. A shame, because practice can make all the difference in public speaking."

> **"Before I speak, I have something important to say."**
>
> —Groucho Marx

Demosthenes, a statesman in ancient Greece known for his great elocution, was said to practice on the shore projecting his voice over the roar of the crashing waves. Some modern speakers have used boom boxes in the same manner to perk up their volume. Rumor has it that Senator Joe Biden improved his articulation by practicing speeches with a mouthful of pebbles.

One of the best ways to prepare for public speaking is to listen to yourself on tape. One expert suggests clicking a toy metal cricket (or frog, if you prefer) every time you hear yourself say "um," "uh," or the like.

"It can also be extremely helpful to watch yourself on videotape, especially in fast-forward mode," says communications consultant Thomas Leech. "It's a great way to discover your funny patterns. A lot of people, for instance, find that they twist their heads from right to left to right in a way that can make an audience dizzy."

Most businesspeople have a long way to go before having to worry about practicing too much, but Leech says it is possible to be over-rehearsed. "Too much rehearsal can make you appear wooden and programmed. That's what happened to Dan Quayle. Everything he did seemed contrived. The public perception was that he had to be heavily coached."

COUNTDOWN TO SHOW TIME

Showing up late for your own presentations could potentially drive your career into a sand trap. In fact, experts say that for any good-sized presentation you should not only arrive on time—but a good half hour or more before your audience shows up.

According to Thomas Leech here's how to best spend those few minutes while the crowd is shuffling in:

Check your props. Make certain that any slides you brought are in proper order. Check to make certain that the overhead is plugged in and working. Test the microphone. "I once saw a company president come before an audience of 300 to present (using an overhead projector) a new software program developed by his company. The audience sat for 10 to 15 minutes while he unsuccessfully tried to get the program booted up. It turned out that he had brought the wrong disk. Check all your gear before going on stage," says Leech.

Invest in liquid assets. On the lectern you should have a glass of liquid, preferably water, to lube your voicebox throughout your talk. Lukewarm water is best because cold can constrict your throat. "Avoid ice—the last thing you need is to choke on an ice cube in the middle of your speech," says Leech. Coffee and alcohol are also bad picks. Coffee can make you need to fly to the bathroom 5 minutes into your talk; alcohol can turn your train of thought into a locomotive wreck.

Belly breathe. Be aware before you stand up to speak of how shallow your breathing has become. You're nervous. Concentrate on breathing deeply, and from your belly. Fatten the belly on your inhales, and collapse it on your exhales. Deep, slow belly breaths can help you both relax and project your words.

Decide to take control. Remember as you prepare to hit the stage that it's your damn show. Someone obviously invited you to speak because you know your stuff. Remember, too, that you're an executive, and you got to where you are for a reason. "At the lectern, be what made you a success and you'll do just fine," says Leech.

AIM BEFORE YOU FIRE

The first step to power presenting is to have a firm handle on your future audience—who they are and what they need. "Being myopic, not looking beyond the corporate view, is one of the biggest barriers to managers giving successful presentations," says Alan Rappoport, a Beverly Hills-based presentation-skills coach to CEOs, presidents, and other senior managers from companies such as IBM, Dow Chemical, and Nintendo. He also coaches sports celebs.

> **"All the great speakers were bad speakers at first."**
> —Ralph Waldo Emerson

"One time, Ernie Banks and I were working on a speech that he was preparing for a group of umpires," says Rappoport. The talk was about artificial turf. The great shortstop had jotted down a list of items to discuss, including turf's effects on a man's knees. "I pointed out to Ernie that knee injury is what players care about—not umpires." What the umps undoubtedly wanted to know, explained Rappoport, was how this glorified patio carpet was likely to affect their calls.

How to avoid speaker's myopia when you don't have a personal coach? "Laundry list everything you know about your subject," says Rappoport. Then examine that list in light of what you know about your audience. Each point you plan to include in your talk should first pass through a filter, says Rappoport. "With every item, ask yourself: 'So what?' 'Who cares?' 'What's in it for them?' If you can't answer those three questions satisfactorily, discard the item."

TALKING TALL—PART II

START OFF WITH A LITTLE APPRECIATION

"Presentations are an opportunity to showcase your abilities, and you never know who'll be in the audience to notice," says Stuart Levine, CEO of Long Island-based Dale Carnegie & Associates, Inc., the popular people-skills training organization. One leadership ability worth showcasing is sincere appreciation, and there's no better time to show it than when you first open your mouth. "It's never inappropriate," says Levine, "to start your talk with the words 'Hello. I very much appreciate your coming here today.'"

HITCH EYEBALLS WITH SOMEONE

You can prepare a speech with language as poetic as Hamlet's soliloquy, but if you deliver it standing as rigid as the White Cliffs of Dover, the event is likely to go over like Shakespeare at a tractor pull.

Communications experts agree that most messages we send are both verbal and nonverbal—and the nonverbal part is the more important. Some studies indicate that the expression on your face and your tone of voice account for 90 percent or more of what you communicate to another human being. The words themselves can be as extraneous as parsley.

The most vital part of nonverbal communication is eye contact. "Making good eye contact is the single fastest way any businessperson can improve his or her presentation skills," says Alan Rappoport. But be aware—not all eye contact is good, he says. "I've seen a lot of lunchtime speaker groups teach that you should pick a point in the back of the room or move your head from left to right like you're running a radar screen. That's bogus eye contact. Real eye contact is random and personal, he says—and an audience knows the difference."

The way to make eye contact real is to eyeball one party in the audience at a time. How long do you maintain eye contact with that one person? "As long as it takes to finish your thought," says Rappoport. Then you move to the next set of eyes. If there are 100 people in attendance, don't think you need to get them all. "Every time you look at one person, you're casting an aura of contact on everyone around him," says Rappoport. "Don't worry, everybody in all sections of the room will think you're talking to them."

Rappoport strongly suggests that you be selective in choosing members of the audience you link eyes with. "Look for people smiling or nodding their heads in agreement. That will help boost your confidence." If your confidence is flagging to the point that looking your audience in the eyes makes you sweat, then look your audience in the middle of their foreheads, suggests Rappoport. "I assure you, they'll never know the difference."

> **"Be sincere; be brief; be seated."**
>
> —*Franklin D. Roosevelt*

KEEP IT SHORT AND ORDERLY

Good talkers never ramble. The best speeches are organized around very specific points—three and no more. "Most of us will forget 40 percent of what a speaker has to say 60 minutes after a presentation. By the end of the day, we'll forget 60 percent. One week later, we'll forget 90 percent. As a speaker, it's foolish to clutter a presentation with 85,000 specifics," says Alan Rappoport. "If you want them to remember anything you said, keep it simple."

Simplicity loves clean notes. Rappoport suggests that you bullet your main points, along with perhaps a few introductory remarks on index cards—and write BIG. White index cards, by the way, are okay, but

Rappoport prefers cards of color. "Use green for your opening, yellow for the middle, red for closing—that way you'll always know where you are." And, should your cards scatter, you'll be able to rearrange them in a snap.

TREAT THE ENGLISH LANGUAGE WITH RESPECT

One thing that can turn any crowd sour is littering every phrase with "um," "uh," "like," or "ya' know." This can be as annoying to an audience as nose-blowing during a flute solo. Yet trashing the English language is a felony committed by many people in business. Fortunately, it's fairly easy to atone.

"If you would only pause, you would reduce this problem by half," says Alan Rappoport. Television, with its breakneck chatter, has taught airwave-bred Americans that there's no room to pause and take a breath, he says. "We think when we pause for a second in public that it's as wide as the Grand Canyon. But for the audience, it's not that wide at all." In fact, says Rappoport, the audience appreciates an occasional break.

REACH OUT AND TOUCH SOMEONE

The last thing a speaker wants to do is grip the lectern like the captain of a ship in a typhoon. According to Alan Rappoport, "Hands have to be in motion if the voice is going to inflect." He invites you to try an experiment. Have a friend say, "I'm mad as hell and I'm not going to take it anymore!"—once with his hands tacked to his side, once with his hands waving about at will. Close your eyes and listen. "You will hear the difference," promises Rappoport.

Not only do hand movements affect your speech, but they also send a forceful message about who you are. Experts say that folded arms across your chest tell an audience that you are not an open person. Hands cupped over your genitals make you look paranoid. Hands locked behind your back give you the look of a Marine.

The most effective way to move your hands—and in fact your whole body—is to do so in a way that is fully natural for you, says Rappoport. "Most business speakers shut down and can't be themselves in front of an audience—they get infected with what I call 'CEO-itis.'" But the most impressive speakers remain free of this rigidity. "If you look at the Perots and the Iacoccas, you'll notice they give you a piece of themselves. They reveal themselves with their body movement and speech," says Rappoport.

It can be hard to reveal yourself if you don't really know yourself, says Rappoport. That's why he often sends his clients on missions of self-discovery. One such mission involves enlisting the help of a friend you normally spend a lot of time with. Ask them to shout "Stop!" every time they see you make a gesture with your hands. Take note. As you focus on those gestures that come naturally to you during the course of the day, you'll learn more about who you are.

Then, next time you're up before an audience, push yourself to use those same gestures. "When you first start this exercise, you'll actually be pretending to be yourself," says Rappoport. "Then it will come more naturally. Once you know what makes you a successful communicator, you can conjure up a better image of your real self. Ronald Reagan studied himself when he was at his best."

George Bush, however, did not, says Rappoport. "He was always balling up his fists at inappropriate moments in his speeches and debates. Once, I remember, he was talking about 'quiet diplomacy' with his fists pounding. You could just hear Roger Ails (the president's speech coach) in the background saying, 'we need to overcome the wimp factor, so look tough.'" It doesn't work when you're trying to be something or someone you're not, says Rappoport.

AVOID THE PITFALLS OF TECHNOLOGY

The days of the bulbous, spongy microphone are numbered. The portable, wireless mike that clips neatly onto a tie or collar is taking over. Thank goodness. The "peanut" mike gives you all the freedom of a cloud.

Should you be stuck with an old-fashioned, nailed-to-the-lectern microphone, however, you'll have to make the best of it. "Twist the microphone and move to the side of the lectern," says Alan Rappoport. "That way your audience can see that you're human."

If you're working with a peanut mike, there's only one caveat, but it's a biggie: Be sure to unclip the little bugger after you leave the stage. Otherwise, you risk the same fate as *Naked Gun* star Leslie Nielsen: Your next trip to the toilet could result in an auditorium of people listening to the sounds of your flushing!

Two other perils of modern technology involve the laser pointer and the overhead. The key to using the pointer, experts say, is to flash it. Once your audience sees what you're pointing to, turn the thing off. Otherwise, any slight jiggle of the hand can create a bouncing dot on the wall that will make your audience think they're at Wimbledon. The key to the overhead is to do like the network weather announcer— continue to face front. Don't make the common mistake of yammering at the back wall while mooning your audience. They won't like it.

Q & A: KEEP THE POWER AT THE PODIUM

At the end of most presentations comes the moment that leaves some otherwise confident speakers wishing they were somewhere safer—like bungee jumping into the Grand Canyon.

Even though few execs spend a whole lot of time prepping for questions, "handling the Q & A is crucial to a speaker's success," says Thomas Leech, a San Diego-based presentations consultant who has provided speaker training to execs at such companies as General Dynamics, TRW, and Magnavox. "One question handled improperly can blow a half-hour speech in seconds."

Leech suggests that managers giving talks in which they expect a Q & A to follow should take a tip from the politicians and enlist coaches beforehand to fire out questions. That way, there should be no surprises.

> **"The play was a great success but the audience was a failure."**
>
> —Oscar Wilde

"Whatever you do during a Q & A," says Leech—"don't get smart, and, no matter how obnoxious a question—don't attack back." "Audiences," he says, "can be like piranhas—you toss a little blood in the water, and things can get savage."

Dale Carnegie's CEO Stuart Levine, who coauthored *The Leader in You*, says that a Q & A gives you further opportunity to showcase your talents. His cardinal rule is to always repeat a question before you attempt to answer it. This serves three purposes: It assures that everyone in the audience heard the question, it buys you time to formulate an answer, and—perhaps most important—it tells the audience that you heard the question. "The ability to listen," says Levine, "is one of the foremost qualities of leadership."

"Another important part of a Q & A is to monitor your body movements," says Levine. "Encourage questions by acknowledging audience members with your palm up, fingers extended. Never point a single finger." And don't snip any questions short with an abrupt palm-out "Yeah-stop-I-got-you" gesture. "You should be encouraging development of thought, not cutting people off midstream," says Levine.

TELEPHONE TACT

SOMETIMES ALL-BUSINESS IS OKAY

There's a time to chitchat and a time not to. "Don't feel compelled to start every phone conversation with 'How are you?'" advises Stephanie Winston, president of The Organizing Principle, a time-management consulting firm.

If you're working on a rush assignment, the last thing in the world you need is for Rosemary in accounting to tell you how she and her husband, Douglas, and the kids, Jennifer and Jason, are doing. It's not at all rude when you pick up the phone and hear Rosemary on the line to say, "Hi, Rosemary, what can I do for you?" And for outgoing calls, says Winston, it's fine to start off with something like "Hi, Joe, I have two brief questions, and I know you're the guy who has the answers . . ."

DIAL WITH DISTINCTION

Unless you're pushing hot dogs on the street corner, the telephone is an integral part of your business. It pays to use it well. Here are some telephone "commandments," courtesy of Marjorie Brody, president of Brody Communications, an international training corporation based in Elkins Park, Pennsylvania, and coauthor of *Climbing the Corporate Ladder*.

Answer on time. Don't make callers wait (or hang up) by letting your phone ring more than three times.

Announce yourself. Let the caller know the right person picked up the phone—use both your first and last name.

Don't play games. It's best to answer your own phone; if you must have someone screen for you, instruct that person to do it tactfully.

Asking "Who is this?" and then responding with, "Oh, well, Ms. Jeffries is not available," is crude. Rather, your assistant should first say that Ms. Jeffries is not available, and then ask who is calling.

Use good diction. Speak slowly and clearly—and smile. A smile will be reflected in your voice.

Identify yourself. When placing a call, say who you are. If you are transferred, repeat your name to whomever picked up the extension.

Check your timing. Always ask "is this a good time to talk?" before launching into your spiel.

Avoid sidebar conversations. It's really ill-behaved to have conversations with someone in the room while you've got some poor soul on the line.

Don't put people on hold. Everybody hates being ushered into the ozone. If you absolutely have to do it, limit it to no more than 20 seconds.

Call back if disconnected. If your communication is cut off, it is the *caller's* responsibility to redial.

Return phone calls promptly. If you can't call back within 24 hours, have someone else call back for you.

Reveal your absence. If you are going to be out of the office for an extended vacation, have your voice mail say so.

KNOW THE RULES OF THE ROAD

The car phone differs from the office phone in more than its mobility. First, the car phone is not a private line, and, therefore, private conversations should not be conducted on the road. "You don't want to announce a secret merger deal to every trucker and ham radio operator in the country," says Marjorie Brody.

Second, realize that the owner of the car phone often has to pay to receive calls. "It is therefore good manners and good business practice," says Brody, "to ask beforehand whether the person you're considering calling would mind occasionally hearing from you on his car phone."

TELEVISION TALENT

DRESS FOR THE CAMERA

The higher you climb the corporate pyramid, the greater the chances that one day you'll find yourself on television. You'll be surrounded by offensively cheery people, someone will yell "Air time!" and—presto—there you'll be chatting up millions of Americans in their easy chairs and underwear drinking Buds and wolfing Doritos.

Television creates new challenges for the business speaker. "You'll need, for instance, to reconsider the way you dress," says Gloria F. Boileau.

"Certain colors change dramatically on camera, and certain patterns will create bleeding (also called smudging or swimming) when they interact with the lines on TV," says Boileau. To play it safe, she suggests a thin pinstripe or solid suit of navy or gray, a solid shirt of either pale blue or pink, and (for men) a red tie. "Small prints on the tie are good—like pin dots or little sailboats. Avoid anything with repeated diagonals."

Boileau also recommends a smidgen of makeup. "If your face is a beacon, no one will hear you speak." Often studios will provide make-up. But you may need to bring your own. "Go to any make-up counter and ask for translucent powder," says Boileau. "Using a puff pad (available in any dime store), you want to lightly buff your entire face and neck—especially those parts that protrude like your forehead, nose, and ears."

SHOW YOUR NICENESS

Why do so many corporate executives get in front of televsion cameras and act as dour as accident victims? "When people see you in an auditorium, they don't expect to like you as much. What they're looking for is sincerity. But people are not going to want you in their living room unless they really like you, unless you are open and warm," says Leslie A. Dach.

"I think Michael (we're talking about Olympia's cousin here) seemed warm enough on television, but he wasn't easy or accessible. People want a president who can be a welcome guest in their home—not someone serious or hard," says Dach. "The same," he says, "holds for business leaders." So today when Dach is working with clients such as execs from the Big Three auto manufacturers, he advises smiles, genial postures, and an earthy manner of speech.

LET'S MAKE A DEAL

There's the little red light—you're on the air. Your first impulse is to say "Hi, mom!" Try not to. Aim your peepers at the host, not the camera. "The TV audience makes a deal with you," like they're peeking at you over a picket fence talking to someone else. If you look directly at them, you make them feel funny." "The only exception," says Alan Rappoport, speaking consultant to top execs at Fortune 500 companies, "is when you are given an earpiece and are asked to address a call-in viewer. Then—and only then—should you gaze into the camera."

Beware also of moving cameras. Don't assume that because you're done gibbering that the camera is no longer on you. George Bush, during his debate with Bill Clinton, made the ruinous error of getting snagged eyeballing his watch. Headlines the next day read "Is George running out of Time?" Don't do anything in the vicinity of a camera that you wouldn't want millions to see on the 10 o'clock news!

5·PROTOCOL

Business is a kind of society. If you don't practice the right manners and customs, you won't be summoned into that society's inner circles. Seemingly little things, like knowing how to ask for a raise, where to take a client for lunch, and how to walk into a colleague's office, turn out, experts say, to be not so little at all.

In this section, business leaders discuss the unwritten rules of greeting, eating, even seating—and more.

As you'll see, the rules of protocol are not as obvious as they may seem—and they change from place to place and time to time. In "Foreign Customs," for example, international executives—from as far away as London, Bombay, and Singapore—will cue you in to some of the unwritten rules of the business road. And in "E-mail Convention," experts speak of how a new technology has created a protocol of its very own.

ASKING FOR A RAISE

DO IT WITH FINESSE

If you're bursting at the seams of your Armani suit to be earning $8,000 more than you do now, you *could* march into the boss and forcefully state your demand. "And chances are about 5 in 100 that you'll succeed," says Mike Deblieux, a human resource consultant in Tustin, California. "In the other 95 cases, making a gruff demand will start a downward spiral."

Better option? "Say to your boss, 'I'd like to increase my base pay by $8,000. What position do I need to attain that, and what do I have to do to get it?'" suggests Deblieux.

KNOW YOUR WORTH

"Before you hit the boss up for a raise, you should get a clear picture of your worth to the company," says Michael W. Mercer, a business psychologist with The Mercer Group in Barrington, Illinois. To get that picture you should be popping in on your boss at least several times a year, asking, "Gee boss, how am I doing?" Also check out compensation surveys, comparing your package to that of others. "Perhaps the best way to give yourself a prereview self-evaluation is to stick your feet into the job pool," says Mercer. "Nothing," he says, "will give you a more realistic picture of the value of your services than to go on a few interviews."

> **"Money is better than poverty, if only for financial reasons."**
>
> —Woody Allen

Of course, once you start comparing your salary to the market rate, you may be surprised. You may find that you're earning far below the industry average. "In that case," says Mercer, "it might be time for the biggest, baddest, boldest gamble you can take on the job: You say, 'Boss, I've got an offer elsewhere for a lot more than I'm earning here—either match their offer, or I'll have to leave.' But don't do this," warns Mercer, "unless you're really prepared to leave—because if you've miscalculated your worth, your boss may suggest just that."

What if your research tells you you're overpaid? Time to rip up the evidence and never utter a word of it to your presumably ignorant boss? Not at all. Use it to your advantage. Say to your boss, "I recognize that the average salary for this job is $50,000 and you're paying me $55,000. That tells me that you value my contributions and that I'm on the fast track in your eyes. Let's talk about how I might make even larger contributions. What do I need to do to get a promotion?"

DON'T WAIT TILL YEAR-END

Waiting until the end of December to argue for a promotion or raise is like waiting for your car to sputter before you pull in for gas. "It's a lot easier to keep your career running smoothly when you regularly give it some fuel," says Mike Deblieux.

Deblieux says that you should remind the boss throughout the year of your progress and accomplishments. He recommends that you whip off regular status reports, either weekly or monthly, and shoot them into your boss's in-basket. "The report can be very simple, even handwritten," says Deblieux. "It should have three columns. Column one should read *Things I'm Working On*. Column two should read *Status* and column three, *Completion Date*.

"Keep it short and sweet," says Deblieux. "List only those things you're working on that are important. Don't list dinky projects."

"By reminding your boss what you're doing, you'll accomplish at least three goals," says Deblieux. First, you'll be reminding the chief what a hardworking soul you are. Second, you'll be making your boss's job easier by helping him keep track of what's going on. ("The more you help him be a good boss, the more he's going to want to do for you," says Deblieux.) And third, by keeping copies of all your reports, you'll have plenty of ammo to help you argue for a promotion at year's end.

BUSINESS CARDS

SPRINKLE THEM AROUND

Make sure your business cards look good, carry them in a classy-looking holder, and use them. Often. "Don't forget secretaries and office administrators—they almost never get business cards, and they really appreciate it when they do," says Marjorie Brody, president of Brody Communications, an international training corporation based in Elkins Park, Pennsylvania, and coauthor of *Climbing the Corporate Ladder*.

Adds Gloria F. Boileau, a California-based communications and image expert whose clients include Rolls Royce, Westinghouse, and the Internal Revenue Service, "The best way to get people to hold onto your card is to write a little note on it. It could be a simple thing like 'Excellent seminar, Jack!'—that could be enough to make someone keep your card for many years."

BUSINESS ETIQUETTE

NOTHING TO IGNORE

"Etiquette counts—not only in fancy restaurants and at English tea parties, but also very much in business dealings," says Marjorie Brody. "It's amazing how many people don't get ahead because they don't exercise common courtesy."

"In fact, *entire companies* can sink or swim on the basis of manners," she says. "Good manners affect employee morale, improve company image, and, over the long run, increase profits." Here are some prime examples of good and bad business manners:

> **"Learn politeness from the impolite."**
>
> —North African saying

Entering someone's office. Don't walk in uninvited. Rather, tap on the door, and stand there until you are invited in. Don't throw your coat down— ask where you can put it. And don't grab mints, a pencil, or anything else off of someone else's desk without asking if it's okay.

Calling names. Use real names, not "honey," or "doll," or "dude." If a person has been introduced to you as "Charles"—call him "Charles," not "Chuck." Similarly, you should not turn "Michaels" into "Mikes," "Bobs" into "Bobbys," or "Susans" into "Sues"—until they've told you that they want you to get that familiar.

Meeting and greeting. Extend your hand and shake. Be firm, but don't crunch. Men: Many of you feel compelled to offer women limp handshakes, often grabbing only their fingers. Know that women don't like wimpy handshakes any more than men do . . . Nor do they enjoy being ignored—extend your hand to a woman just as you would to a man; this isn't the 1950s—treat all hands the same. And make certain that yours are never wet—wipe them on your pants if you need to, but make sure your palm is parched before squeezing it into someone else's.

Making introductions. Do it—even if you forget a name or title. It's better to be seen as forgetful than boorish, says Gloria F. Boileau. The proper protocol, in case you've ever wondered, is to first introduce the younger/junior person *to* the older/senior. It's also customary to first introduce a colleague from your company *to* a client or customer.

Gossiping. Don't.

COMMUNICATION CHOICES

KNOCK WHENEVER YOU CAN

Business communications sure were easier back in the old days. If Lou Grant needed to summon his associates, he'd hang his head out of his office door and holler, "Hey, Mary. Hey, Murray." That was that. Today, we have our choice of voice mail, e-mail, fax, personal memo, knocks on the door, gorillagrams, you name it. What's best?

"It depends," says Carol Rudman, a Long Island-based management development trainer who works with companies such as Motorola, AT&T, and American Express. "To avoid depersonalization, I'd go in the direction of face-to-face whenever possible, followed by telephone, followed by e-mail. The written memo on a piece of paper is the least personal mode of communication."

"Granted, there are times when a certain medium is best, personal or not," says Rudman. E-mail is obviously the quickest way to go if you need to copy lots of people quickly.

"But I would avoid e-mail, memos, or even the telephone in situations where there's any kind of strong emotion, where nonverbal communication may play an important role," says Rudman. "For any kind of negotiation, for example, I'd want to be able to see the person."

CONFLICT RESOLUTION

EMPLOY TIME-HONORED TOOLS

There are tried-and-true protocols for dealing with conflicts among colleagues—and they do not include hurling each other's laptops out the windows. Below are some considerably more productive conflict-resolution tools, from Jon Weiss, executive director of the Center for Conflict Resolution in Chicago.

- Always focus on the problem, not the individual.
- Keep talking. "A lot of times people stop talking and just make assumptions about the other party that often turn out to be wrong," says Weiss.
- Be receptive to solutions other than your own.
- Stick to your interests and needs, rather than your principles. For example: Instead of saying *It's terribly unprofessional and rude of you to come late to our meetings*, say, *When you're late to these meetings, I find that we wind up having to repeat what was said when you weren't here, and that slows things up considerably.*

DANCING OVER THE BOSS'S HEAD

FOR THOSE VERY SPECIAL OCCASIONS

When it comes to business protocol, going over your boss's head is somewhat akin to a loud belch in a fancy restaurant. If you can help it, you don't do it.

"There are, however, times when circumventing the chain of command may be a rational move," says Sandra K. Allgeier, director of human resources for Providian Corporation, a financial services company based in Louisville, Kentucky. A few such circumstances:

- If you catch wind that your boss is doing something unethical or asking you to do something unethical, report this. In a larger company, contact the head of the internal audit department or the director of human resources. Some organizations even have a chief ethics officer. In a smaller firm determine who is the highest ranking official that you can access.

- If you and the boss have a serious disagreement over a work issue, you may delicately suggest that the two of you schedule a chat with his boss. This is risky, of course. Chances are good that he'll feel threatened. "On the other hand," says Allgeier, "it will be less threatening than his finding out *after the fact* that you flew over his head."

- If you are working on an assignment that higher level managers have expressed an interest in, are asking questions about, then you might want to copy them on status reports, correspondence, and the like. Generally, this is fine to do if you start out doing it from the beginning of a project. Most organizations have unwritten rules about what is acceptable and not acceptable in this regard; ask around to find out. You might find you can bend the rules a little if you have reason to attract your boss's bosses' attention to a problem.

E-MAIL CONVENTION

DON'T LET IT ZAP YOUR HIDE

It's like magic. Press a button on your keyboard and your message appears instantaneously in the offices of thirty or forty colleagues. In some instances, however, e-mail can work like black magic. "I've noticed several negative phenomena with e-mail, and I've seen some people potentially hurt their careers with it," says Peter Blackford, director of the export division at Goodyear Tire & Rubber in Akron, Ohio.

First, says Blackford, too many people are taking advantage of the impersonality of e-mail to say things that they would probably never say to anyone else face-to-face or even by phone. "There's a tendency with e-mail to be easily caustic or sarcastic," he says. "The same rules of courtesy and good taste that apply elsewhere should apply to e-mail." Remember that e-mail communication doesn't offer the same nonverbal or tonal clues that a live conversation, or even a phone conversation, does. Things meant to be funny or sarcastic may be taken as deadly serious.

"Second," says Blackford, "too many people are getting routed messages—people who really shouldn't or needn't be. It's so easy to copy people with e-mail that there's a tendency to overdo, clogging people's electronic mailboxes and wasting everyone's time—or worse. Any message that is at all critical of a person's performance should be a private matter—not e-mailed to the entire world," says Blackford.

Third, the speed of e-mail is making for very sloppy communications. You should also take time to construct your e-mails using proper English. "I find it really annoying to get e-mails that have poor sentence construction, misspellings, and no paragraphs," says Blackford.

PITY THE POOR READER

One can presume that when our grandparents were first introduced to the telephone, they made mistakes—perhaps yelling into the receiver or speaking too softly. So it is with e-mail today.

Experienced e-mailers will tell you that it is not okay to type in all caps—novices often do it, and it is referred to as "shouting." Even more vexing to e-mail readers is having to deal with mile-long lines that need to be scrolled in order to be read. "Think about your screen as a page—and don't go over the margins," says Peter M. Saunders, director of the Rauch Center for Business Communications at Lehigh University in Bethlehem, Pennsylvania. "If you have a system that flags runovers, pay attention to the flags"—just as you would the ping of a typewriter.

A few additional tips for making e-mail more productive:

- Try to provide meaningful subject lines to your message. It will be helpful, and appreciated by those who get lots of messages on their computer.
- Don't ask for receipts unless you really need them. If everyone does it as a matter of course, it can slow up the whole networking system.
- Regularly clear out your e-mail. Too much clutter in your computer can create hassles when you're trying to find a particular message.

FAXING FRUGALITY

---◆---

MAKE ONE PAGE SUFFICE

Dear Ms. Ellis:

Attached is the schedule of events that I promised you on the phone this morning.

Sincerely,

Benedict Geraci

Come on, Benny. Ms. Ellis can *see* that the schedule of events is attached. Unless she's completely senile, she can also remember from this morning that you promised it to her on the phone. Why waste her time reading, your time writing, and our world's forests by creating two extra sheets of paper (your copy and the recipient's) every time you send a simple fax?

"You don't need cover letters. They don't make sense, economically, environmentally, or any other way," says Kay duPont, owner of The Communication Connection, an Atlanta-based consulting company specializing in helping leaders in business and government to become better communicators.

And what if Ms. Ellis works in an office with many people who share the same fax machine? "All you need to do is write her name at the top of the main page," says duPont. "It's very simple and very quick."

FOREIGN CUSTOMS

FITTING CONDUCT CAN CLOSE DEALS

You arrive at the airport on your first international assignment. You want to win some profitable contracts, naturally. You also don't care to make a fool out of yourself. But business customs do vary from culture to culture. Below, a few pointers on doing business abroad from James Reinnoldt, Northwest Airlines' regional managing director for Southeast Asia and Greater China, based in Singapore.

Business cards. Be ready (without fumbling) to produce a business card when you meet someone in the Far East. After receiving one, scrutinize it for about 10 seconds. When seated at the table, place the card or cards in front of you.

> **"In Paris they simply opened their eyes and stared when we spoke to them in French! We never did succeed in making those idiots understand their own language."**
>
> **—Mark Twain**

Gifts. Both a potential crisis and an opportunity. Be tastefully subtle. In Asia, it's customary to give something of value, but consumable or functional—such as a nice pen set, or (in non-Islamic countries) a good bottle of whiskey. One universally accepted gift (even better than alcohol) is a box of golf balls with your company logo on them. Ensure that all gifts are nicely wrapped.

Be careful of symbolism when gift-giving, though. "I know of someone who brought a beautiful Swiss knife from Zurich to Bangkok as a gift to a supplier," says Reinnoldt. "To the Thais, a knife (or scissors) means the breaking of a relationship. In this case, a bottle of scotch would certainly have been better." If you have any question about the appropriateness of a gift, ask your hotel's concierge. A good concierge can not only advise what to give, but can also arrange for its purchase and wrapping.

Ups and downs. "In Buddhist countries you'll find the people have respect for the top of the head as the holiest part of one's spirit," says Reinnoldt. "Things of value and respect are therefore placed on a high level." For example, photos of the King of Thailand are always displayed near the ceiling, and images of the Buddha are placed on a high shelf. To put something like that on a lower plane would be disrespectful.

"I know of one American businessman who concluded a deal in Vientiene, Laos, and agreed to prepare the contract. After writing the body of the contract, he affixed the signature lines with his own on one line and that of the cosigner just below it. Two weeks later he received the contract back, torn in half, with an angry note saying how insulted the cosigner was by this brash act of disrespect (putting one name above the other)," recounts Reinnoldt.

Footware. If you are ever so lucky to be invited into an Asian's home, remove your shoes as you walk in the front door. This also applies to some Japanese restaurants.

APPRECIATE NATIONAL DIFFERENCES

No, people in Latin America don't speak Latin. Warsaw is not an insurance company. And Brussels is more than a sprout. Many Americans are a little weak in their social studies, but if you're going abroad on business, it pays to bone up. Some people take it as an affront when you know zilch about their homeland.

For example, "each nation in Europe has its own distinct culture—we are NOT a federation of similar little countries. This may seem obvious, but it is the most common error made by U.S. visitors to Europe," says Theo Clarke, principal consultant with Tignosis Limited, a management consulting firm based in London, England, that specializes in cultural change and the introduction of new technologies.

Business culture can change dramatically crossing a border, says Clarke. For example, "Brits and Germans tend to get terribly irked if anyone comes late to a meeting. Walloons (French-speaking Belgians) are more understanding. And the Greeks, Italians, and Spanish tend to be most casual about timekeeping." Similarly, says Clarke, "learning patterns differ widely . . . Germans want to know every detail (never skip a slide in a presentation to Germans). Italians want just the broad concepts, asking for details only when they need them."

A discussion of the many cultural nuances in each country of the world would fill volumes. For now, just a few examples from Clarke of how the British tend to do business a little differently from others:

- The English use irony frequently. Be aware that the speaker may mean exactly the opposite of what he is saying.
- English business relationships can be more informal than those in other countries, such as Germany and the United States. Brits tend to include more humor in their meetings. Americans and Germans concentrate more on the job at hand.
- In Britain, praise is usually the prerogative of bosses, as opposed to in North America, where business people praise each other more frequently.
- Brits are not as swift to reveal personal feelings in conversation. This is not because they are unfriendly, but because they have a greater sense of privacy.

KNOW THE RIGHT MOVES

It's your first business trip to India. You've put together a masterful sales presentation. You feel crestfallen when your prospective customer shakes his head from side to side. Don't be! "In India nodding means no, and shaking the head sideways means yes—a common source of confusion for newcomers to our country," says Sunder Kimatrai, home office representative for Twentieth Century Fox in Bombay.

That's far from the only example of how body language can differ radically from one country to another.

In Japan, of course, the bow is more common than the handshake (the lower you go, the more respect you convey). In India, a common greeting is to bring the palms together into the "Namaste" position. In South America, business acquaintances often greet with a robust hug. And in many countries, bringing your thumb to your index finger (the North American "okay" sign) is the most obscene gesture you could make.

Lastly, always remember on your business lunches in India to handle food with your right hand. In a country where toilet paper is a rare commodity, the left hand is the one designated for personal hygiene. (You will find a small mug next to the toilet that is used for water.) "It is not considered appropriate to touch food with the left hand," says Kimatrai.

ATTUNE YOUR ENGLISH

As an American business traveler, you may find it a relief to go to a place like England or Australia. No more putting your tongue into traction. Everybody there speaks English—right? Well, yes, it's English they speak. But English mutates when it crosses oceans. And if you're not sensitive to those mutations, you can wind up, well, making a bloody arse of yourself.

Just ask he-man Hulk Hogan. He wound up on a British talk show (they call them chat shows over there) and was asked by the interviewer what he was wearing around his waist. Hulk responded, "That's my fanny pack." The audience and interviewer were taken back. In Britain, "fanny" is a word for a woman's genitalia. He should have said "bum pack."

Protocol

In the world of international business, such blunders are commonplace. For example:

- "In 1974, I was a vice-consul to the British Trade Development Office in New York City when a British exporter of clothing asked us for help introducing to the U.S. market a line of ladies underwear. He proposed to label them 'Gay Panties.' He was advised against it," recalls former consulate official Roger Dixon.
- David J. Butcher, an accountant who runs his own outsourcing and consulting business in Lingfield, Surrey, England, recalls one of his first business trips to the States. "I got asked after dinner whether I wanted a cordial. I said 'excuse me?'" Back home, he explains, a "cordial" is a non-alcoholic, sugary drink made from fruit and water.
- And Theo Clarke, principal consultant with Tignosis Limited, a London-based management consulting firm, warns that even the simple word "quite" can be misunderstood. "In Britain 'quite' lessens the adjective to which it is applied—it is not synonymous with 'very.' Thus, to tell someone that he is 'quite good' is to call him mediocre," says Clarke. "I saw one American trainer completely lose the goodwill of his British audience by making this mistake. I advise Americans to avoid the word 'quite' entirely."

Other examples:

- In England, if someone says he'll "knock you up" in the morning—relax. It simply means he'll be calling on you...And if he offers to bring a "rubber," that only means an eraser!
- Tell a Brit that you are "pissed," and he'll assume you had too much to drink.
- In South Africa, if you are told that something will be done "just now," don't hold your breath. In local lingo it means sometime in the future . . . maybe . . . if you're lucky.
- Automobile-talk presents boundless opportunities for misunderstanding . . . In England, hoods are called "bonnets," fenders become

"wings," gasoline is "petrol," and a trunk becomes a "boot." In India, however, the trunk is often called a "dicky."

- Food-talk can get awfully confusing, too. In England, french fries are called "chips," dessert becomes "sweets," and cookies are "biscuits." In New Zealand, however, cookies are often called "biccies."

LEARN AS YOU GO

Where can Americans go for advice on local customs abroad? "The first stop in each country should be the American Chamber of Commerce. Chamber people are often very willing to help," says James Reinnoldt.

In most countries you'll also find local books that explore all the variations of cross-cultural interaction. "For example, throughout Asia," says Reinnoldt, "you can find a series of books entitled *Culture Shock Singapore*, *Culture Shock Japan*, and so forth."

"Another good source of information would be a local foreign students association. The majority of universities have one," says Reinnoldt. "Not only will most foreign graduate students be happy and willing to give advice, but they can also help arrange great contacts!"

LUNCH MANNERS

---◆---

THE ART OF MEALING AND DEALING

Many a deal has been done over tuna sandwiches and chef salads. A good number of deals have also been cracked before the bread. To make the most of your business lunches, observe a few simple guidelines from Marjorie Brody.

- **Choose a familiar place.** By dining at a spot you know, there are less likely to be unpleasant surprises. Do, however, run the name of the restaurant by your guest; she may be a vegetarian who would not appreciate Big Bubba's House of Beef.
- **Set a time limit beforehand.** Suggest to your guest that you convene for lunch "between 12 and 2," or whatever. By setting a time limit, you avoid the later awkwardness of one party wanting to sit and sip espresso while the other desperately needs to bolt.
- **Don't order anything sloppy.** No lobsters, crabs, onion soup, spaghetti, corn-on-the-cob, or burgers with extra ketchup and mayo.
- **Start with small talk.** Don't try to discuss anything serious until the meal has been ordered. You want to allow time for your guest to read the menu and for the server to greet you.
- **Eat politely.** Just in case you forgot: The food goes to your mouth, your mouth doesn't go to your food. Napkin goes on your lap. French fries are not finger food.

> **"Nothing is less important than which fork you use."**
>
> —Emily Post

- **Grab the tab.** The one doing the inviting should be the one doing the paying. Slip the waiter your credit card either before the meal comes (if you're a regular) or as you order your coffee.

OFFICE PRESENCE

SKIP OUT AROUND THE CLOCK

Great leaders focus on results. They don't dictate to others in painful minutia how to achieve those results. Alas, not all bosses are great leaders. Some managers seem to care more about "face time" in the office—getting in by, say, 8 a.m. and staying till 6:30 p.m.—than they do about the actual work that gets done. Yes, it's idiotic. Yes, it's perverted. Yes, it's depressing as hell to have to put up with such an imbecilic demand. But there are ways to get around it.

Discuss the problem. Don't bring it up in a confrontational way, but you can bring up the issue of face time. A good venue would be during a staff meeting. You might say something like: *Some of us were talking about how there seems to be an overemphasis on hours worked, but it seems that what should be more important is how much work actually gets done. Perhaps we could brainstorm ways to work more effectively that do not involve unnecessary hours in the office?* "Who's going to argue with that?" says Sandra K. Allgeier.

> **"Big brother is watching you."**
>
> —*George Orwell*

Share literature. Drop articles on the boss's desk that discuss the need for meeting the diverse needs of the workforce. There are many articles (and case studies) that discuss how allowing for flexibility and freedom can boost productivity, employee morale, and retention of personnel.

If your efforts to reason are unsuccessful, you'll need to resort to the following measures:

Protocol

Take longer lunches. Or run out for several short spells during the course of the day. Depending on your circumstances, and the office culture, it may be quite easy to slip in and out.

Head for home. "It is the strangest thing," says Allgeier, "but I have seen people 'work at home' without any negative repercussions, in fact, with great support, where leaving the office before 6 p.m. is not acceptable."

Set a deadline. If the boss's attitude is more than you can stand, you need to ask yourself how long you're going to put up with it. Set a date at which point you will reevaluate your need to seek opportunity elsewhere.

POWER SEATING

IT PAYS TO GET TO THE MEETING EARLY

Indian chiefs of old who wanted to communicate power wore more feathers on their heads than the other braves. Lions roar louder. And little kids often shove. In the business world, communicating power is often (but not always) a more subtle affair. "One way to communicate power is by grabbing the right seat at the meeting," says communications and image expert Gloria F. Boileau.

According to Boileau, the person at the head of the table clearly has the most authoritative position. It's also an unwritten rule that the boss gets to sit there. But all the other spots are usually open for grabs, Boileau notes. At a table for eight, the other most important locations, she says, "are at the foot of the table and the center seat on either side—where you have a clear line of sight to the big cheese at the head of the table."

6·PRINCIPLE

At a televised hearing before Congress, a pack of tobacco executives testified before the nation that nicotine isn't addictive—a scientific absurdity akin to saying that water isn't wet. Those tobacco execs have completely lost their moral compasses.

In this section, experts address the issue of integrity—and how to exercise it in the daily conduct of business. You'll see that on numerous happy occasions doing the right thing—treating the elderly well, behaving with respect to the environment, speaking truth to the public—can have a glowing effect on a business's bottom line. And whether there are dollar signs attached to it or not, acting with integrity will always help you get a sound night's sleep.

We wrap up this section with an entry on how to spot others who may be acting with less than total integrity. Given the presence in this world of the kind of people who testify that nicotine is just the cat's meow, this entry is a must-read.

AGE DISCRIMINATION

REAP THE REWARDS OF EXPERIENCE

Many potential employers of the elderly, as well as some of the elderly themselves, have bought into the notion that the aged are slower, can't learn, are fragile and often get hurt on the job, and other miscellaneous bunk. "Research clearly shows that the adage 'You can't teach an old dog new tricks,' is garbage," says Catherine D. Fyock, president of Innovative Management Concepts, a Kentucky-based management consulting firm whose clients include Hardee's Food Systems, AT&T, and Hallmark.

Fyock should know. In her past position as director of field resources for Kentucky Fried Chicken Corporation, she was instrumental in the development of KFC's national initiative for employing older workers. She is also the author of *UnRetirement: A Career Guide for the Retired . . . the Soon-to-Be-Retired . . . the Never-Want-to-Be-Retired.* "The truth is that older adults take fewer sick days and tend to be more loyal, conscientious employees," she says. "As a group, they also tend to value diplomacy, tact, and courtesy, and, therefore, make wonderful employees for positions that involve customer contact."

"Furthermore, since people with a few wrinkles are more likely to know what they want to be when they "grow up," older workers tend not to job-hop as much as younger people," says Fyock. She cites Ryder Truck as one company that enjoyed a much lower turnover rate when they initiated a program to hire older workers for part-time driving positions.

"Advertisements geared toward attracting older workers should target the interests of the elderly," says Fyock. For example, a recent campaign by Hardee's shows an obviously retired gentleman looking bored stiff, leaning on his golf clubs. The caption reads, "Tired of being retired?"

Principle

BIGOTED BOSSES

REAM 'EM

___

If the boss doesn't seem to like you, and it's clear that the reason has to do with the color of your skin, your sex, national origin, religion, age, or a disability, then keep good records of any telling comments and behavior.

If you are fired, demoted, or penalized in any way—and you can draw a case that the boss's behavior was related to his bigotry—then the last laugh will be yours. Call the lawyers at the Equal Employment Opportunity Commission, and they will descend on your place of business like the Marines at Iwo Jima. The toll-free number is 800-669-4000.

Although there are no federal laws, some local governments also offer protection from discrimination based on sexual orientation.

ECO-INTELLIGENCE

CASH IN ON ENVIRONMENTAL ACTION

It's uncanny the way environmental consciousness at work can pay off not only in the obvious and important ecological ways, but also in financial ways," says Craig Ronai, president of Ecologic, a consulting company specializing in the creation and operation of "green" businesses.

Just a few examples:

Separate your waste. By separating your aluminum, glass, and colored and white paper, you put less stress on your region's landfills. "You also save money," says Ronai. "A lot of companies pay to have their garbage picked up. If you sort your garbage, however, recyclers will almost always come and take it away for nothing."

Change bulbs. Compact fluorescent lightbulbs are enormous energy-savers. A 26-watt fluorescent bulb gives off as much light as a 100-watt regular incandescent bulb. *And* it lasts about ten times longer! "Although compact fluorescents were once very expensive, the price has come down considerably," says Ronai. "And with rebates being given by many power companies, they are often cheaper than regular bulbs—and sometimes even free."

Use both sides. Making two-sided photocopies saves trees and cuts your paper costs in half. Using two-sided *recycled* paper is an even better bet.

Save your peanuts. Styrofoam peanuts and other packing material from incoming boxes can be stored and used to pack outgoing boxes. You save, the planet gains.

Work at home. Consider working at home if you have the option, and encourage it throughout your business. "Staying home cuts auto emissions, saves money on transportation (and likely food and clothing, as well), improves quality of life, and, in many cases, can boost job productivity. A very nice package," says Ronai.

Read up. "There are many eco-intelligent moves you can make around the office," says Ronai. For additional information, he suggests picking up a copy of *The Nontoxic Home & Office*, by Debra Lynn Dadd, or *50 Simple Things Your Business Can Do to Save the Earth*, by The EarthWorks Group. He also recommends ordering a catalog or two from companies that offer environmentally benign office supplies, such as Seventh Generation in Burlington, Vermont (800-456-1197).

ETHICAL DILEMMAS

DO THE RIGHT THING

Integrity, or lack thereof, is where many people in business win, lose, or draw themselves into corners. There's no balancing act here. The people you're working for won't respect you if they don't think they can trust you. (Even if they're liars and crooks themselves.)

What is integrity? "It's drawing a line between right and wrong and knowing on which side to stand," says Thomas Horton, past chairman of the American Management Association.

But what if your boss *orders* you to do something unethical, like push a load of worthless penny stocks on a hapless client? "Tell him you can't and explain why. If the two of you can't resolve it, ask your boss to accompany you to talk to his boss," says Horton.

Most employers will be reluctant to force you to do something unethical. Conversely, once you've shown that you're willing to acquiesce to such requests, you may find yourself getting them with increasing regularity.

OFFICE ROMANCE

PROCEED WITH CAUTION

Any number of articles and experts will tell you to avoid office romances. The truth is, however, that it's an awfully difficult thing to do. It's estimated that half of all relationships today start in the workplace. Unless one of you is already married—which is nearly always a recipe for a host of disasters—office romances can be sweet, and they don't have to interfere at all with your career. Nor do they have to result in charges of sexual harassment.

You do, of course, have to follow a few simple rules:

Move in very slowly. You may be steaming to get physical, but never make an advance early in a relationship. Wait to know each other at least a few weeks, preferably a few months. Build a foundation of friendship before you attempt to become lovers, says Riki Robbins Jones, popular author and speaker, and an expert on gender issues and social relations.

Hint, hint, hint. Before you zero in on your would-be paramour, throw out a few innocuous questions to find out just how receptive he or she might be to a new relationship. Try, for example, "Are you seeing anyone?" or "How's your social life?"

Check the hierarchical chart. "Dealing with subordinates today is very dangerous, you're really putting yourself on the line for a sexual harassment suit," says Jones. "Going for the boss, on the other hand, has *always* been fraught with danger. If and when you have a falling out, your job will definitely be at risk." By far the best option, obviously, is to stick to your peers.

BE HONEST BUT DISCREET

You and your colleague down the hall have discovered after months of furtive glances and shy smiles that you can't remain just colleagues any longer. You're now lovers. Should you tell the world?

If employee relationships are against company policy, as they are in some corporations, you'd better not tell a soul—"rumors of romance spread like the bubonic plague," says Jones. "But if it's okay with company policy, then it's fine, actually preferable, to acknowledge publicly that the two of you are an item," she says.

But that doesn't mean you should walk down the hall arm in arm or smack each other playfully on the backsides outside of the company cafeteria. Strive for professionalism. "The office is not a place for open intimacy," says Jones. "Never inflict your sexuality on colleagues. It will embarrass them and you will very likely lose their respect."

PERSONAL VALUES

JOSTLE YOUR CONSCIENCE

How did the modern world get so full of Ebenezer Scrooges, people who, in the name of Almighty Profit, treat others with indifference or disdain, firing employees on a whim, cheating customers, poisoning the air? It's not that unscrupulous businesspeople never had scruples—"it's more likely that they had, but those scruples were lost somewhere along the line," says Richard Kinnier, associate professor of counseling psychology at Arizona State University.

> **"If I don't acquire ideals when I am young, when will I?"**
>
> —Maimonides

Old Scrooge had the prodding of three Christmas spirits to help him shed his "bah-humbug" attitude and recoup his personal values. Unlike the Dickens' character, you're on your own to recapture and keep any lost principles. You can, however, use the following tips to help guide you:

Broaden your horizons. "People with distorted ideals often find each other and use each other to reinforce those ideals," says Kinnier. Look at any number of cult groups (some of which forbid contact with outsiders). "You'll tend to be in much better touch with your own true values if you make a point of regularly breaking out of your little clique," says Kinnier.

Test your positions. Use other people—preferably people you respect, but outside of your clique—to test your beliefs. "Say to them, 'this is what I believe'—then invite them to attack that belief," says Kinnier. "I'd think if the tobacco executives were to ask, say, their grade school teachers or class nuns what *they* thought about selling addictive substances to children, these people might consider changing careers."

Although it doesn't work as well, "you can also try to attack your beliefs on your own," says Kinnier. "Have a conversation with yourself in which you act as both attacker and defender. If it helps, use two chairs and move from one to the other."

Confront your own mortality. "Scrooge broke down and cried when the Ghost of Christmas Future pointed out his grave to him. It was at that point that Scrooge realized that life means more than money, and greed was not what he wanted to be remembered for," says Kinnier. "Thinking of death has a way of rapidly returning us to our core values."

Sleep on your decisions. "If you're sitting on a decision that challenges your principles, give it time," says Kinnier. "Sometimes sleeping on a decision will give you a fresh perspective, one that is more clear and true to your inner beliefs."

RACE RELATIONS

DON'T PRETEND YOU DON'T NOTICE

Admit it. Even though you feign nonchalance, the fact that your boss or a colleague is of another race is something of which you are painfully aware. You sometimes feel awkward, uncertain if anything should be said about your obvious difference in shade.

> **"We must learn to live together as brothers or perish together as fools."**
>
> —*Martin Luther King, Jr.*

"Hypersensitivity to race is an unfortunate by-product of our history and culture, and it's something we shouldn't feel guilty about, nor should we sweep our feelings under the carpet," says Alan Weiss, founder and president of Summit Consulting Group, Inc., based in Greenwich, Rhode Island.

Some pointers on working in a multiracial environment:

Don't wonder about terminology—ask. "I've seen white people go to incredible lengths to describe someone—who happens to be the only black man in the building—as 'the tall thin guy . . . you know . . . with the dark curly hair, and the striped blue shirt . . .' That's silly," says Weiss. "It's perfectly all right to mention a person's race. If you don't know what that person would like to be called, go ahead and ask." Some blacks prefer "black," others prefer "African American," and others like "people of color." Most Asians now consider "Oriental" to be pejorative, just as most Native Americans dislike the word "Indian."

Beware of cultural gaffes. It happens often in interviews, says Weiss. The interviewer will ask questions such as "What kind of music do you like?" or "What hobbies do you have?" If the candidate is of another race, the impression may be had that the interviewer is trying to decide whether he'd fit into the predominant culture. It's better to narrow the questions to past and present job performance or to ask questions related to the current job opening . . . *This job involves lots of travel. How do you feel about that?*

Don't stereotype—even if positive. All Asians are natural whizzes at science and math. On the surface, not a bad thing to say. But such a stereotype, even though it is positive, risks doing harm. One particular Asian, for instance, may be much better suited for sales or advertising than working in R & D, yet he may get coerced into R & D because someone in the organization believes that "they" are just so darned good at science and math. "Be careful of 'they-isms,'" says Weiss.

OCCASIONALLY TAKE A POLL

The plight of being a manager is that you are often out of the loop. If, for example, you were the supervisor of a multiracial workforce, would you know it if there was racial tension on the floor? Perhaps. Perhaps not. "If you want to find out for sure, you'll need to bring it up—and I would recommend doing so once or twice a year," says Keith Weigelt, associate professor of management at The Wharton School.

"I'd do it in person in front of the group, rather than by memo. I'd talk about the issue in very general terms, without pointing anyone out. I'd want everyone to know that if there were any problems whatsoever stemming from differences in race, religion, or gender, that I'd like to know about it," says Weigelt. "This is obviously a first step toward any solution—you can't fix a problem that you don't know exists."

SEXISM IN THE OFFICE

NEEDED: VIGILANCE AND OBJECTIVITY

Sexism comes in many forms. When someone is hired or fired, promoted or demoted, praised or demeaned, based on whether that someone is male or female, that's the worst kind of sexism—the kind that is not only unprincipled, but also illegal.

Other forms of sexism won't get you on the FBI's Most Wanted list—but that still doesn't make them right. For example, men who display images of women with pouty lips and proud bustlines should consider the effect of this on the opposite sex. "Those images—which can play into old sterotypes of women as playthings—may appear in film presentations, company literature, or calendars," says Billie Wright Dziech, professor at the University of Cincinnati and a popular speaker and writer on the subject of sexism and sexual harassment. "Men may not understand the discomfort that those images can cause to some women."

Some women, on the other hand, may not understand how tough it is to be a man today—forever afraid of being labeled sexist for something as innocous as opening a door for a female colleague. "A lot of men today feel that they can't win—that they can't ignore or address the issue of sexism in a way that will satisfy everyone," says Jeffrey Kahn, psychiatrist and president of WorkPsych Associates, a Manhattan-based management and mental health consulting firm. He asks that women judge men individually and fairly—and not solely by their gender.

SHARING CREDIT

BE A GOOD TEAM PLAYER

Senior managers tend to hold in high esteem those who are strong team players. "I've seen junior people come through who didn't want to share the answers they've found with other people. I can't respect that," says Bill Flister, senior vice president/regional manager for Chase Manhattan Bank on Long Island. "What impresses me is someone who is available and helpful to other people."

Thomas Horton, says that in his many years in corporate life he came to recognize early the signs of a good team player. One such sign is giving credit where due. Team players don't hog all the glory. "Give credit whenever you can, and do it in public," says Horton. "If you can do so honestly, give a little credit to your boss, too."

> **"It isn't necessary to blow out the other person's light to let your own shine."**
>
> —*Confucius*

Besides being the decent thing to do, sharing credit makes you look more like management material. At a time when most of your colleagues are either trying to protect themselves or cover it with glory, you'll be moving away from self-centeredness and recognizing the value of other people's work. Compliment your fellow workers, and your boss will see in you someone who is more concerned with honest productivity than star status.

SOCIAL RESPONSIBILITY

LOOK TO *TWO* BOTTOM LINES

Doing good for the world isn't only good for your soul, it can be good for your checkbook, too. "Companies and individuals who make a positive contribution to society will be most likely to prosper in the long run," says Clifton S. Sorrell Jr., president and CEO of The Calvert Group, Ltd., a diversified investment management firm specializing in holdings of companies that make profits by solving global problems.

> **"How wonderful it is that nobody need wait a single moment before starting to improve the world."**
>
> —*Anne Frank*

Looking to make a contribution to your world? Want to make career and business decisions to benefit humanity? Sorrell suggests using the following adaptation of the criteria for social responsibility used by the Calvert Social Investment Fund:

- Produce products and services that sustain, rather than destroy our natural environment.
- Do not discriminate on the basis of race, gender, religion, age, disability, ethnic origin, or sexual orientation.
- Do not support or collaborate with repressive regimes.
- Take no part in the manufacture of weapons or weapons systems.
- Encourage participation throughout the organization in defining objectives.
- Negotiate fairly with workers.

- Offer employees stock ownership or profit-sharing.
- Provide an environment supportive of employee's physical and mental health.
- Foster awareness of a commitment to human goals, such as creativity, productivity, self-respect, and responsibility—within the organization and without.

In addition: Consider subscribing to *Business Ethics*, a magazine about making money in a socially responsible manner (located at 52 South 10th St., Minneapolis, MN 55403); and *In Business*, a magazine about environmentally sound business (419 State Ave., Emmaus, PA 18049).

SPOTTING LIARS AND CROOKS

IT GETS EASIER WITH PRACTICE

Unless you work with only saints, chances are you've been lied to on the job. It may have been a little lie (*Mr. Adams is in a meeting right now*), a medium lie (*the check is in the mail*), or a big lie, the kind that devastates honest people and good companies (*these chemicals are safe as can be; this investment is a sure thing*). Just because there are plenty of liars in fancy suits out there doesn't mean you have to do business that way. You do, however, have to be able to recognize the con merchants so that you can steer a wide path around them.

Fortunately, most liars shed clues. If you learn how to read them, you could save yourself and your company much grief. Here's a lesson in spotting lies from John W. Kennish, former police officer and now a safety and security consultant based in Westbrook, Connecticut.

Study the person. It's harder to lie to your mother than to a stranger. That's because she knows you so well. Moral: While you're making chit-chat with someone you've just met, pay careful attention to little mannerisms. You want to establish that person's "normal profile." Most people go into a defensive mode when they start lying, says Kennish. "If you know how that person is when not lying, you're more likely to notice the subtle differences in behavior, speech, and body language when there is lying."

Get cozy. It's much easier to lie to someone on the telephone than in the same room. It's harder yet if that person is right in your face. Move in close to someone who is trying to sell you something. Maintain strong and direct eye contact. If he's lying, you want to make it so difficult for him that sweat starts to ooze from every pore.

Look into the eyes. People who lie tend to look away. Or, on the contrary (because they've heard that liars often look away), they may try to stare you down. Watch for a faster eye blink rate and for the eyes to open wide—especially to the point that you can see white on each side and below the iris. "Such signs are extremely evident in the films of President Nixon during the Watergate press conferences," says Kennish.

Watch the mouth area. "The lips and nose are particularly stress-sensitive," says Kennish. "Watch for the hand to suddenly move to scratch the nose or lips or to cover a faked cough. A hand to the mouth in conjunction with a fake cough often reveals a subconscious attempt to obstruct a lie." Watch also," Kennish says, "for lip biting, or lips that suddenly press tightly together. Some liars will actually hold their lips together with their fingers," he says.

Other clues that someone could be lying to you include:

- Voice takes on a higher pitch
- Speech speeds up
- Excess smiling
- Clammy hands
- Finger drumming
- Frequent repositioning of body
- Deference overkill (calling you "sir" or "ma'am," even though you're still young)

7·POWER

As first-time managers in today's business world know all too well, you're usually expected to fly off the seat-of-your-pants. One day you're an accomplished salesperson, accountant, buyer, programmer, whatever. The next day somebody is calling you boss. There's little time for transition; no time for education. It's often fly or crash.

Where can you turn for advice? In no other area of life—except perhaps investing—is there more bad advice to be found. Anyone and everyone, it seems, knows how things ought to be run.

In this section, you'll find leadership advice not from anyone and everyone, but from some very sharp business pros. You'll get invaluable insights into how to pull off with grace such management duties as hiring, motivating, leading meetings, fostering teamwork, and—if absolutely necessary—firing.

No, reading the following entries won't make you a great leader—but will, hopefully, set you off in the right direction. It'll then be up to you to use your power or abuse it.

ACTING LIKE A LEADER

SEVEN SIGNS OF TRUE AUTHORITY

A leader can (and often does) make or break an organization. What differentiates a "maker" from a "breaker," a good leader from an oaf who just happens to be occupying a corner office? Here, according to John Clizbe, senior partner with Nordli, Wilson Associates, a New England-based group of management and consulting psychologists, are seven attributes of successful leaders:

1. **Vision.** "Any good leader will have a strong sense of purpose and be able to convey it," says Clizbe.

2. **Theme.** A theme is what people associate you with, which in an effective leader will be the relentless pursuit of the vision. For example, Franklin D. Roosevelt's theme was clear: *We're going to offer a New Deal to take care of people.* Lee Ioccoca's theme was clear: *We're going to recover—no matter what.* Ross Perot's theme was clear: *We, the 'outsiders,' need to get control.*

> **"A leader is a dealer in hope."**
>
> —*Napoléon Bonaparte*

3. **Trustworthiness.** "People won't follow you unless you have shown integrity and consistency," says Clizbe.

4. **Modesty.** "The most powerful leaders I know see themselves as supporting their employees—rather than having their employees work for them," says Clizbe. "When they speak of their work relationships, they say so-and-so and I work *together*, rather than so-and-so works for me."

5. **Coolness.** "Good leaders don't run around like the world is about to collapse every time there's a problem—they send off vibes that read 'we can work this out,'" says Clizbe.

6. **Clearness.** True leaders simplify matters; they don't complicate.
7. **No airs.** The best leaders know who they are, and they don't try to be something or someone they are not. "Harry Truman comes to mind," says Clizbe.

IT'S A MATTER OF SKILL

"A leader is, above all else, a person who can communicate and motivate," says Stuart Levine, CEO of Dale Carnegie & Associates, Inc., the popular people-skills training organization. "The most important part of communicating is *listening*," he says. And the most important part of motivation is *giving recognition*. "There are leaders at every level of the organization—don't think you have to be the CEO in order to practice those skills."

GENERAL CHARACTERISTICS OF A WINNER

Horror tales abound of managers who jet off for two days to the latest quickie "leadership" seminar, return back to home base, and force-feed their staffs with some newfangled management theory that they picked up from one of the speakers. Those who survive to tell the tale know that there are true leaders, and there are people who run around with kooky beliefs, leadership cliches, and fast "solutions" to problems that only seem to result in problems growing bigger.

"Leadership," says Colin Powell, America's former top military man, "is the art of accomplishing more than the science of management says is possible."

That doesn't mean that the science isn't important. You can probably administer more effectively if you're up on the latest management research. But it's important to remember that employees are people—and few people take warmly to the idea of being "managed." Perhaps the best investment of your time, rather than trying to follow every management fad, is to keep a close eye on those you consider true leaders. Note their attributes, their characteristics. Don't try to become these people—always be yourself—but do attempt to assimilate their best traits.

What you'll probably notice, says Marvin C. Patton, major general, United States Air Force (ret.), are some of the following qualities:

Dignity. "Good leaders are dignified—but not aloof," says General Patton. "As an officer, I wouldn't hesitate to sit down and have lunch with the men, but I would never play poker for money with them or go to a stag party."

Respectfulness. "If you show respect for people, most will respect you," says General Patton.

Motivation. If you yourself aren't motivated, and if you don't show your motivation, it's going to be awfully tough to instill motivation in a group.

Sensitivity to human needs. True leaders aren't so rut-minded to think—and behave—as if people work only for paychecks and monetary bonuses. They know that people need positive feedback, a sense of purpose, and a feeling that they are in control of their own destinies.

BRAINSTORMING BASICS

MAKE LIKE FREUD

As the leader of a brainstorming session, your mission is to encourage the group to come up with great ideas, right? Perhaps. In the end, yes, what you're looking for is great ideas. "But *telling* people to come up with great ideas is going to encourage nothing but stage fright," says Marsh Fisher, cofounder of Century 21 Real Estate, now heading IdeaFisher Systems, Inc., a computer software company in Irvine, California. Instead, he says, "ask your fellow brainstormers simply to come up with free associations, from which great ideas will flow."

> **"The best way to have a good idea is to have lots of ideas."**
>
> —Linus Pauling

"You don't build a bridge by going right from point A to point B. The first thing you do is amass your materials—the cement, the steel, the rivets . . . ," says Fisher. "It's the same with effective brainstorming—you start with associations." In other words, your mission is to encourage everyone in the group to throw out words and concepts—related, however loosely, to the project at hand.

For example, say you're leading a brainstorming session to come up with an ad campaign for a new red lipstick. You might start by asking for everyone's associations with the color red. Things might start off slowly, they usually do. Someone will say *apple*, another person may say *blood*, and another, *tomato*. "The best ideas usually come later in the game," says Fisher. "That's when you'll start to get unusual associations like *cocktail sauce, Santa Claus,* and *Lucille Ball.*" These are the raw materials from which you may come up with a few great slogans.

MAKE LIKE KING ARTHUR

When you want to create a team concept, to have people working together comfortably and creatively, make sure to provide them with comfortable chairs—and seat them at a round or oval table. "It's a simple concept that can make a big difference in how well people work together," says Gloria F. Boileau, a California-based communications and image expert whose clients include Rolls Royce, Westinghouse, and the Internal Revenue Service. "The round table creates the most equal feeling, as opposed to the classic rectangular table that can create a very hierarchical feel," she says.

DELEGATION DO'S AND DON'TS

DEAL RESPONSIBILITY AND WALK

There is, perhaps, no greater morale killer, no greater source of humility, frustration, and anger in the office than having to deal with a boss who gives you responsibility one day and then unceremoniously yanks it away the next. Good leaders, obviously, don't do this.

The best leaders "set a course, do strategic planning, lend a personality to the business, delegate—*and then keep their hands off*," says Henry Bloch, chairman and cofounder of H&R Block, North America's largest tax preparer. "Even when you know someone is doing something wrong—don't intercede," says Bloch. "Making mistakes is the only way that people learn and grow."

GIVE THE NOVICE A CRACK

You've got that extra little project that isn't going to make or break the company and two ways you can delegate it. You could give it to Maryanne, who's done a million of these projects and is juggling several dozen at the moment. She'll resent you for it. Or you could give it to Sam, who may not get it perfect, but who would love to try. He'll thank you profoundly for the opportunity.

"People want to grow, to expand their potential," says Laura Henderson, president and CEO of Prospect Associates, a health communications and biomedical research firm based in Rockville, Maryland. "I had one woman who was a great scientific writer, but she wanted to learn graphic art. When a simple project came along, I had her work in the graphics department for a while. She was ecstatic."

If you really, really delegate wisely, you'll ask Maryanne (who has always wanted to get some hands-on management experience) to oversee Sam's work. That way, your delegation of a simple project winds up as a learning opportunity and a motivating force for *two* people.

FOSTERING TEAMWORK

IT REQUIRES MORE THAN A MEMO

Of *course* you want everyone in your department to work cooperatively. But what can you do to make it happen? Some business leaders issue "Let's all pull together" memos every couple of months, close their eyes, and hope for the best. Inevitably, nothing happens. Other leaders may go so far as to divide people into "teams," without changing anything else about the way the business operates. Inevitably, nothing happens.

Fostering teamwork with people reared in a largely dog-eat-dog world requires some radical steps, but steps that when they are taken, lead decisively to happier people and greater productivity, argues Alfie Kohn, popular lecturer, scholar, and author of numerous books, including *No Contest: The Case Against Competition.*

Here is what Kohn recommends:

Look for cooperators in the first place. "Managers should hire, in part, on people's attitudes about cooperation," says Kohn. "Look for candidates who express an interest in working together with other people, rather than beating others out."

Clear the path. "You cannot promote any sense of community if one person's success has anything to do with another's failure," says Kohn. "No true teamwork will occur," he says, "in corporate environments where, for example, the review process allows only a certain percentage of the individuals to get a bonus or high ratings in any given year." (Kohn doesn't much like the idea of group bonuses, either—see page 163.)

Develop a culture of trust. Check in your local area for workshops devoted to the development of trust—and enroll the group. Often, such workshops will involve outdoor, cooperative challenges, such as crossing a foot bridge or maneuvering through an obstacle course.

Model cooperation. "To talk of working more cooperatively so that the team can clobber other teams (within the company or without) is to miss the point entirely," says Kohn. "You can't foster true cooperation if everyone is still talking competition. Rather than focusing on clobbering anyone the team should focus on excellence," says Kohn.

Communicate. At the end of the team's first project together, and periodically thereafter, encourage discussion of how things went. What went well? What can be done better? What can we do differently next time?

HIRING THE BEST

HARVEST RIPE CANDIDATES

Newspaper classified ads are the singles bars of the hiring scene. Go into them once, and you'll rapidly discover how hard it is to find a satisfying match.

"Despite its popularity, running newspaper employment ads is one of the least effective means of attracting good people to your door," says Catherine D. Fyock, president of Innovative Management Concepts, a Kentucky-based management consulting firm whose clients include Hardee's Food Systems, AT&T, and Hallmark. The problem with newspapers is that they don't target your market. You may get oodles of responses, but they'll come from a hodgepodge of humanity, largely unemployed, who have nothing in common except that they spend their mornings drinking coffee and reading "Help Wanted" pages.

Here are some sourcing alternatives that are often much more effective and cost-efficient—sometimes even free!

Direct mail. Lists are available from many sources. Consider particularly professional organizations and specialty publications lists. Members and subscribers can often be broken down by business title, company size, geographic location, or other criteria.

Telephone. From direct mail lists you can also get phone numbers. Calling prospects is a time-consuming alternative, yes, but one worth considering if you're in a tight labor market. That personal touch can really help bring in good people.

Information seminars. You put on a seminar offering free education. For example, one temp agency in Atlanta did a free seminar for women on job hunting. At the end of the show, they put in a pitch for their agency and hooked up with several excellent workers. If your seminar is free and worthwhile, churches and community centers will often give you space at no charge.

Realtors. Some real estate brokers offer relocation services (both formal and informal) to help trailing spouses new to town. They appreciate hearing from you.

TV and radio. Not only an excellent medium for targeting your market, but also sometimes less expensive than newspapers. If you can hook up with your state employment agency, TV and radio stations may run your help wanted notice as a free public service announcement!

Agencies. Head-hunting firms have typically cost employers big bucks (often 30 percent of the first year's salary). But recent years have seen a rise of agencies offering "unbundled" services. For instance, you can work out an inexpensive deal where the agency supplies you with the leads, but you do the contacting and cajoling.

LOOK FOR PASSION IN THEIR EYES

As an employer, the laws of supply and demand, at least for the time being, are clearly in your favor. Advertise a semidecent wage and offer adequate health care, and the world will beat a path to your door. Opening that door, you'll find a gaggle of earnest wannabes, all in clean pressed outfits, with crisp résumés on heavy-grade, off-white bond. Who do you pick for the job?

"The best employees are those with passion, those who feel so strongly about what they're doing that if you didn't pay them, they still might do the job on a volunteer basis," says Laura Henderson. In Henderson's business, that often means looking for people with a big interest in health issues.

Ah, but how do you know if the interest an employee expresses in your business is genuine? "You ask lots of questions and look for consistencies," says Henderson. Among the questions Henderson asks are ones about volunteer activities and likes and dislikes of previous jobs.

She also finds it helpful to set up hypothetical situations. . . For example, *Let's say you were asked to develop a brochure for low-income women with ovarian cancer—what might the focus be?* "I'm interested not only in what the person's strategy might be, but how much excitement there seems to be in developing it," says Henderson.

"I interviewed a woman recently for an accounting position—her face literally glowed when she was talking about setting up a new accounting system. I knew at that point that she'd be the right person for the job, and I was absolutely right," says Henderson.

BEWARE OF HYPE

Résumé inflation—can you spot it? What exactly does it mean when a candidate says he was "responsible for" boosting revenues by $3 million or "credited with" reducing manufacturing costs by $2.5 million?"

"I always ask very detailed questions about a candidate's past assignments, and then I listen very carefully to the answers," says Osamu Yamada, general manager of WKKJ, a Japanese branch of a Hong Kong-based manufacturer of electronics equipment. "I listen in particular to the amount of detail given to me." If the candidate lapses into vague generalities, that, says Yamada, "is a good sign that he's exaggerating about his accomplishments."

COVER YOUR ASSETS

One criminal-minded employee in a sensitive position can crash an entire business. It happened to Britain's 232-year-old Barings bank when a 28-year-old option trader in Singapore zapped *$1.4 billion.* It can happen to your business. How can you know if that smart-looking candidate sitting across the desk from you intends to walk away with much more than a paycheck?

You can't. But you can check to see if that person has a history of such conduct (and whether he's being truthful when he tells you on his application that he has no such history). "A basic background check really doesn't take a lot of time or effort," says John W. Kennish, former police officer and now a safety and security consultant based in Westbrook, Connecticut.

See the cops. In most places you can obtain police records on applicants. The normal process is to obtain a consent form at the police station and have the applicant sign it, authorizing you to be given access to his local police record, if any. With the form signed, the police will hand you a list of any felony or misdemeanor convictions.

Check litigation history. You may also want to check up on the applicant's civil litigation records, which you or the applicant can obtain from the county courthouse. "Do you really want to hire someone who has sued four previous employers?" asks Kennish.

Examine credit problems. The local courthouse can also tell you if the candidate has ever declared bankruptcy. And any bank can refer you to a credit agency to check someone's history of paying off debts. (You'll generally need the applicant to sign a release.) "Past financial problems may foreshadow future ones," says Kennish, "if someone has a history of running away from his financial responsibilities, that may also tell you something important about that person's character."

Look over the wheel. If the applicant will be driving for the company it is *imperative* to get his or her driving record from your state department of motor vehicles. "If you hire someone with a past DWI (driving while intoxicated) arrest, and that person goes out and runs someone over, *you've* got major liability," says Kennish.

HISTORY'S LESSONS

LEARN FROM THE BEST

Yes, there were managers long before there were MBAs. *Someone* had to manage those massive constructions such as Stonehenge, the Pyramids, and The Great Wall. Expeditions to new lands also needed planning and administration, financing and bookkeeping, and good public relations. Winning wars, of course, requires leadership as well as weaponry. Throughout history, in other words, there have been senior managers, middle managers, shop stewards—and just like today, these leaders were good, bad, and so-so. What lessons are to be learned from their triumphs and mistakes?

Below, a few insights from modern-day organizational experts reflecting on managers of yesteryear:

- The Confederacy didn't lose the Civil War for lack of good generals. In fact, it boasted the best, including Jebb Stuart and Stonewall Jackson. Both were known for their down-to-earth leadership—in fact, they often dined with the common soldiers and slept in the outside air with them. "The best leaders, like Stuart and Jackson, lead by example more than by directive. They don't carry around a 'holier-than-thou' attitude," says Keith Weigelt, associate professor of management at The Wharton School. "Many of today's managers with their special perks, reserved parking, and 'I'm top dog' mentalities, create an unhealthy 'us versus them' work environment, which winds up hurting productivity."
- On the other side of the Mason-Dixon Line, the man in charge proved to be a masterful leader. In Abe Lincoln's torn America, some people backed the strict interpretation of the Constitution, which said

that white men were more worthy than black men; others held dear the Declaration of Independence, which said, "All men are created equal." When Lincoln spoke at Gettysburg and said, "Fourscore and seven years ago," he showed which side of the debate he was on, by referring—very obliquely—to the year of the Declaration. "Had he come right out and condemned the Constitution, he would have offended some people, and then people wouldn't have followed him. But he was much too sensitive and subtle for that," says Edward Donley, former chairman of industrial giant Air Products and Chemicals, Inc. "Lincoln's understanding of people and their sensitivity is what made him perhaps our greatest president—those same qualities make for a great leader today."

- Much closer to the present, Donley cites another American president as possessing certain traits worthy of emulation. "Ronald Reagan certainly didn't have the subtlety of mind that Lincoln had, but he was an effective leader," says Donley. "A large part of his success was due to his relentless pursuit of a few simple principles. He never departed from those principles, never paid much attention to other issues." Those who are successful, in either politics or business, says Donley, "are not devoted to the issues of the hour or the day. They have a concentrated focus on a few goals—and nothing can divert them from that."

MOTIVATING THE TROOPS

MAKE EVERYONE FEEL WHOLE

Judging by how many people express their deep desire to dip their bosses' private parts in sizzling grease, it is quite obvious that many managers and business owners are not motivating but breeding discontent. It doesn't have to be that way.

"There is a desperate yearning in the heart and soul of workers for spirit, purpose, passion, and a sense of meaningfulness," says Virginia Littlejohn, CEO of The STAR Group, an international marketing and consulting firm. "The motivating manager makes people feel like they're working on the equivalent of the Apollo space program," says Littlejohn. "You want to capture people's dreams, give them something to get up for in the morning, give them a feeling you're reaching together for the stars."

> **"I can live for two months on a good compliment."**
>
> —Mark Twain

Here's how to accomplish that:

Cherish input. Show all people—even those who work in the mail room—that their ideas matter. One way of doing that is to set up suggestion boxes. They can be the old-fashioned pencil-and-paper kind or electronic ones. But they must be *interactive*. If people feel that their suggestions are going into a deep, black hole, they'll only feel angrier at you for having wasted their time. Everyone who makes a suggestion should get, at the very least, a thank you note from a corporate officer.

Make work relevant. A key to creating a feeling of teamwork and pride in any organization is to give every employee a good understanding of what the final product is and how it benefits people. It is, therefore, an excellent idea to occasionally bring real, live customers in to meet people in different departments, perhaps invite those customers to company picnics and parties.

Show thankfulness. Give heartfelt thanks to those doing a good job. Praise specific actions like a great idea or a successful project's completion.

Be straight. Many companies today tie praise, bonuses, and promotions to workaholism—although they'll feebly try to disguise it as something else, something vague, like "professional excellence." Rewards that are given out only to those who put in 10+ hours a day will only drag morale to knee-level.

PROVIDE VOLUNTARY EDUCATION

Giving staff ongoing opportunities to learn pays off doubly: You wind up with people who are more capable and more motivated to do a good job. But problems arise when managers coerce people to attend courses, says Paul Jackson, director of Creating Results, Ltd., a management consulting and training company, based in Bath and Bristol, England, whose clients include Oxfam Campaigns and Hewlett-Packard.

"Ensure that anyone participating in a course or a program wants to attend," Jackson asserts. "Anyone sitting there with reluctance is going to be a pure energy drain and will make the first session or sessions tremendously difficult. On the other hand, if everyone is happy to be present, the work usually goes well."

In order to encourage attendance, Jackson suggests some tasty advance communication, advertising the virtues of the course. "Such communication," he says, "might include an interesting quote or two, or a brief personal quiz to whet the appetite." The course can also be presented as a fast route to future attractive projects.

Should you be the moderator of a training program and suspect some people are there not entirely of their own accord, "it's best to give participants a chance to express their misgivings at the very beginning," says Jackson. "Nerve-racking, yes—but worthwhile. Allowing people to vent clears the decks for learning," he says.

POWER VISION

LOOK FOR THE UNUSUAL

In 1986 a small article in the back of the *London Times* revealed that the Soviet Politburo had decided to allow the development of high-definition television. In those days, that meant permitting satellite transmissions into the U.S.S.R.—quite a shocking move back then, for Soviet society had been tightly shut off from the rest of the world.

With that information, Andre Alkiewicz advised his clients, including President Reagan's White House, that the Communist regime's days were near over. "People laughed at us," says Alkiewicz, founder and managing partner of Perceptions International, a Connecti-cut-based corporate consulting firm spe-cializing in the early identification of world changes.

> **"I skate to where the puck is going to be, not where it has been.**
>
> —*Wayne Gretzky*

Of course, Alkiewicz got the last laugh. And as his many clients, including AT&T and a bevy of financial service companies have discovered, the man has an uncanny way of seeing into the future. This is no small talent to have in the business world. "Making a big profit on a trend only happens if you spot that trend before it becomes a trend," says Alkiewicz.

The way to do that, he says, is to "keep your eyes and ears open, looking in particular for anything out of the ordinary." When you spot an anomaly, ask yourself whether it is an anomaly that will remain as such, or whether it will become the norm of tomorrow. For example, when you first saw a woman police officer twenty or thirty years ago, it probably struck you as odd. Had you thought about it, you might have envisioned a coming world with women soldiers, firefighters, and truckdrivers, such as we have today.

The way to forecast change in society is not so much by spotting things out of the ordinary and extrapolating, but rather by identifying the root cause—the philosophy—behind such an anomaly. For example, the philosophy behind the Politburo's allowing for satellite transmissions was one of openness. The philosophy behind women police officers is equality and fairness to women. These were the root causes for those changes. They were also the forces behind major world changes.

Today, says Alkiewicz, to cite another example, we are noticing a growing interest in solar-powered and electric cars. You could extrapolate and try to guess what cars might look like in twenty years and stop there. Or you could look at the root cause, the philosophy behind the change—society's concern for clean air and stable climate—and you can envision major changes of all sorts, from how we heat and cool our homes to our manufacturing processes to our recreational activities.

PROJECT MANAGEMENT

BE A LEADER, NOT AN ASSIGNER

Projects are to departments what calculators are to slide rules. They've clearly become the more modern way of getting things done. That's because they're a more effective way of instituting change. At some point in your business career, you'll be associating yourself more with a particular project than with a specific department—count on it. Someday, if that day hasn't come already, you may even find yourself sitting on top of a large, multi-staffed project.

At that point, you have two choices: You can be a project assigner, and muddle and scrape your way miserably toward the project's completion; or you can be a project leader, and run a crisp, creative, and happy operation that yields a tremendous product at the end. Here are a few essential pointers on the ins and outs of project management from project-pro Barry Greene, an associate partner with Andersen Consulting:

Round up the gang. "You have to organize teams around projects, not projects around teams," says Greene. That is, assemble your staff so that you have the best possible mix of talents—exactly those talents needed to do the task.

Set clear expectations and goals. Make sure you have received painstakingly clear directions from upper management about what is expected out of your project—and make certain that you relay those expectations to the entire team. Let them know what you'll be doing and how. "A lot of managers don't give projects enough up-front thought. They seem to say to themselves, 'we'll figure this out as we move along.' Bad thinking," says Greene. "If everyone on the team knows exactly what is expected from the get-go, they're much more likely to figure out how to get it done."

Communicate the effect. For morale, don't only communicate what the project is about (for example, developing a new software program that will help doctors diagnose a certain disease), tell the team what the impact of the project will be (for instance, potentially saving 4,000 lives a year).

Set parameters. Every project needs to be well-defined in terms of the work that will be accomplished and the time frame within it will be accomplished. "What often happens is that teams are pulled together for a specific project, but after a while they become more of a department, with people working on all kinds of things. That's a mistake," says Greene.

Share your values. At the onset, let people know that this will be a cooperative deal. Everyone should know that you want free sharing of information and mutual support and respect among all members of the team.

Allow for intermediate goals. Some projects may require months, even years. "To keep people motivated you need to set up steps along the way with which to mark your progress. The long-term goal of project completion always has to be kept in mind," says Greene. "But you can't expect people to work and work for eons without seeing anything tangible."

Celebrate victories. When you do succeed at fulfilling an intermediate goal, take time out to reflect on your success. Have a party. Go out to lunch. Or simply stop work and give yourselves a round of applause. Greene recommends making public (cooperative) successes public, but keeping private (individual) successes private. "If one individual does a superlative job, go into his office and congratulate him personally with a handshake or pat on the back," says Greene. "I think that's appreciated much more than the 'Let's have Bob stand up on stage and feel terribly embarrassed,' routine."

EMPOWER THE DESERVING

Official hierarchy be damned! Maximum efficiency results when the person who knows the most about the topic at hand is heading the show. Sometimes, even though you may be *technically* the boss, you'd be doing everyone a favor to just step aside.

"If we need to get something Xeroxed and out the door in a hurry, the Xerox operator will be the boss," says Laura Henderson. "Maybe I'll wind up as the one punching the holes, and if I don't get it right, I'll do it again.

"New people are sometimes shook-up by the way we manage projects around here, but it works. It really works," says Henderson.

REWARDS AND INCENTIVES

GIVE BONUSES THAT MAKE SENSE

There's no question that compensation can change people's behavior. But how? Obviously, if you're the one in charge, you want to compensate people in a way that ultimately boosts morale and benefits the bottom line. Here, according to Keith Weigelt.

Reward strategically. Many a basketball team has fallen from grace because one guy winds up getting all the glory; he feels like king; his teammates feel like serfs; and before you know it, you don't have a team anymore. "Figuring out compensation schemes is complicated—you have corporate goals, division goals, team goals, and individual goals. As a manager you need to think about your strategic objectives and make sure that your compensation plans match them," says Weigelt. At times, he says, "that may mean rewards for groups of people working together, rather than the more common, often simpler, but sometimes simple-minded individual rewards."

Be clear. The best bonus plans offer people objective, quantifiable measures for performance. Compensation schemes that rely on such things as "quality of performance" usually fall apart or leave people feeling confused, sometimes embittered. Bonus plans, says Weigelt, "should wherever possible be based on tangible goals."

Look ahead. A common American business practice is to reward people for short-term achievements. This is usually a mistake, "leading to decision making that may actually hurt long-term performance," says Weigelt. "Bonuses almost never are geared to the long-term, but they should be—three to five years down the road would be a reasonable time frame."

CONSIDER THEIR ABOLITION

The majority of business experts in America, such as Keith Weigelt, believe in offering rewards to employees who meet certain objectives. But some experts strongly disagree. Alfie Kohn, says quite bluntly, "Incentive plans don't work, never worked, and can't work."

Those who disapprove of incentive programs don't object to money. What they object to is the carrot-and-stick approach to motivation used in most North American companies (as well as in most schools). "To summarize 70 studies," Kohn says, "the more you reward people for doing something, the less interest they'll have in doing it."

In other words, *true* motivation, the kind that results in long-term, quality work, must come internally—"from pride and finding meaning in one's work," says Kohn. "Setting up external rewards, like bonuses, only undermines productivity in the long-run by getting people focused on tangible gain. The more people come to work every morning thinking about money, the more harm done."

Rewards can succeed at getting people to do something, admits Kohn. So can punishments. "But the *desire* to do something, much less do it well, simply cannot be imposed," he says. "It is, therefore, a mistake to talk about motivating other people. All you can do is set up certain conditions that will maximize the probability of employees developing an interest in what they are doing."

What kinds of conditions? The most important are what Kohn calls the "three C's" of motivation—*collaboration, content,* and *choice:* Collaboration refers to a sense of true teamwork and cooperation. Content refers to the opportunity to do meaningful work. And choice is the condition that allows workers to determine for themselves how to best carry out their tasks.

And what about that "C" so revered by the masses—*Cash?* "Nothing whatsoever wrong with cash," says Kohn. "It just shouldn't be pushed in people's faces as a contingent reward for doing their work." Rather, he says, "people should be paid generously and equitably. Do your best to make sure they don't feel exploited. Then you should do everything in your power to help put money out of their minds."

RUNNING THE MEETING

ALLOW FOR DEMOCRACY

Running a meeting is both a science and an art. Depending on the nature of the subject and the crowd in attendance, you might want to adjust your style. Whatever you do though, don't get so wrapped up in orchestrating that you forget why you're there—to share ideas. "And sharing ideas involves giving your thoughts, and getting the opinions of others," says Henry Bloch, chairman and cofounder of H & R Block.

> **"A committee is a group that keeps minutes and loses hours."**
>
> —Milton Berle

"Too many discussion leaders get carried away leading; basking in the limelight; listening to themselves talk, talk, talk; that they wind up play listening, not really hearing what others might have to say," says Block.

That's a big mistake. "I think the key to getting the most out of meetings is to have some humility," says Bloch. "If you express that you want things one way and everyone else in the room says that they want them another way—they're probably right."

SQUASH ANARCHY

Every meeting has one, the clown who wants to talk about delicious apples when everyone else is talking navel oranges. Your job, as leader, is to gag him. Nicely, of course.

"You need to figure out the core objective of the meeting, to summarize it clearly for the group, and to make sure that things don't drift around. You need to keep control," says Edward Donley, former chairman of Air Products and Chemicals, Inc.

So what do you do with the stooge at the other end of the table who is still yakking on about those stupid delicious apples? "Very politely point out to him that that subject is not on the agenda for the day, and suggest that perhaps he might want to organize another meeting at another time to discuss his particular agenda," suggests Donley.

TERMINATING WITH TACT

BE GENTLE, HELPFUL, PREPARED

Getting rid of someone who isn't working out is one of the toughest things a manager has to do. Sometimes, however, when a job and an employee are just a rotten fit, there may be no way out. If you're a coward and a cad you can go about it the old-fashioned way, with a pink slip in the mailbox on a Friday afternoon (or the new-fashioned way—by e-mail message). But if you're interested in keeping that person's dignity intact, protecting the morale of the other employees, and going home with a clear conscience, then read on.

"If you fire people right, they'll think they resigned," says Laura Henderson. The trick, she says, "is to apply some smart diplomacy."

Provide a hand. As soon as it becomes evident that things aren't working out, you want to bring the employee in for a counseling session—at least that's how you want it to appear. You might say, "You seem unhappy, John. Apparently this isn't the right place for you. I want to help you to find the right place." The next step might be to outline a five-year career plan with John, walking him through it so that he sees for himself that he and the company are a bad fit. "Continue counseling him—right out the door," says Henderson.

Give selected feedback. "If you know that someone considers himself to be superb in one area, don't bother telling him that he's not—he won't believe you anyway. Find other things to talk about," says Henderson. "Always question whether the information you're giving is going to be helpful, or if it's only going to make the person angry and hurt."

Stay on your toes. If all goes well, the terminated employee will walk away actually feeling good about herself—hopefully moving on to a place where she'll be happier and more effective. If all doesn't go well, you may have to deal with some ugliness. The worst case scenario, of course, is that the employee gets violent. It's best to have security keep an eye on your office when dealing with a potentially dangerous person. How can you tell? "Erratic behavior, flights of fantasy or grandeur (I had one employee who had awarded himself a Ph.D., a J.D., and an M.D.), or a general sense of being out of touch, are all signs I'd look out for," says Henderson.

8·PEACE

"Rich or poor," someone once said, "it's good to have money." Truer words are hard to find. But there's more to work than money, and there's more to life than work. In this final section, the experts talk to us about career in its broadest sense, as a very important part—but a part nonetheless—of a successful (happy, healthy, meaningful) life.

So, if you're dragging yourself to work every morning, or if you have to drag yourself home in the dark every night, you've come to the right place. If work is destroying your happiness, your health, your self-esteem, your friendships, or your family life, then there's valuable counsel here for you.

BALANCING ACT

CONSIDER SIX POTENTIAL SANITY-SAVERS

If the demands at the office, combined with domestic chores, leave you with little time for something called *life*, if the situation has got you angry and depressed and headachy much of the time, if you're searching for answers but aren't sure where to look, start here.

Don't try to do it all. Pay someone to clean your house and cut the lawn. Order from take-out restaurants rather than cooking and cleaning. At work, delegate whatever you can.

Get flexible. If your company doesn't have flextime, argue for it, suggests Susan Averett, assistant professor of economics and business at Lafayette College, in Easton, Pennsylvania.

Work at home. Even if you can swing working at home only once in a while, it can save a lot of commuting time. Many people (but not all) also find that they are much more productive working at home. Remember: Tell others that you are "working at your home office," rather than "working at home." A subtle difference, maybe, but "home office" has a better ring to it.

Take the kids to work. Many companies today have on-site day care. If yours doesn't, it's time to ask why not. If you now cart the kids off to day care at the other end of town, taking them to work with you

> **"The five most stressful jobs are: U.S. president, firefighter, senior corporate executive, Indy class race-car driver, and taxi driver."**
>
> —*American Demographics,* August 1995

can cut down considerably on your transit time and increase the time spent together.

Share the job. Job-sharing—two people splitting the responsibilities and pay of one job—isn't quite common yet, but the opportunity exists in some companies. You might want to start with the personnel department to find out what company policy is, and then approach your boss. "You won't know unless you ask," says Averett.

Swap careers. Not all careers are created equal where it comes to making demands on people's time, Averett points out. Management, law, and journalism are traditionally among the most demanding. Careers that often allow for more reasonable hours include teaching, physical therapy, counseling, and nursing. Did you know that a nurse anesthetist, with one year of post-college training, working roughly a 40-hour week can make well into six figures?

CALLOUSNESS IN THE WORKPLACE

DON'T TAKE IT SITTING DOWN

We all need positive feedback and an occasional "thank you" for work well done. Some need it more than others. If you're one who needs a lot of kind words or just a few that you're not getting, "it's perfectly okay to mention that to people you work with, like your boss," says Carol Rudman, a management development trainer who works with companies such as Motorola, AT&T, and American Express.

"Give people suggestions about how you like to be treated," says Rudman. That "jerk" of a boss who never gives you the time of day may not mean to be a jerk; she may simply be overwhelmed with her own work and life. Telling her that you could use more feedback may be enough to get her nose out of her belly button and get you a little well-deserved recognition.

On the other hand, you may discover she really is a jerk. In that case, says Rudman, "look around and you'll probably discover that she's treating everybody the same—and there's no reason to take anything she says, or doesn't say, personally."

STAND UP TO BULLIES

Like it or not, some workplaces go beyond being insensitive; they are downright *mean*. (If you're lucky enough not to know what office meanness looks like, see the movie *Glengary Glen Ross* with Jack Lemmon and Al Pacino.) "In situations where employers abuse their employees, the interpersonal dynamics as well as the level of emotional pain can be strikingly similar to domestic abuse cases," says Robert Jaffe, a Los Angeles-area psychotherapist specializing in helping people who have been abused.

"In both situations one person starts ruling by fear, and the other buys into it by feeling more and more powerless, less and less in control," says Jaffe.

Some employees go on for years, even decades, dealing with bosses who humiliate, embarrass, and threaten them. They may walk around feeling continually victimized, till one day they explode into pieces, or a stress-related disease forces them to retire—sometimes from work, sometimes from life itself. Obviously, says Jaffe, "there are much better alternatives."

Get a grip. As much as you may have convinced yourself that you are dependent on your present employer, that's not the case. There may be no quick alternatives to giving up your present job, but there are always alternatives. It's helpful to think of yourself not as an employee at all, but as an autonomous contractor whose employer is merely an important client. "Your goal is to change your mind-set so that you begin to see yourself as independent, good at what you do, and capable of finding work elsewhere," says Jaffe.

Make an appointment with the boss. To get out of your victim role you need to get assertive. You need to tell the boss that you don't like the way you've been treated. It will help if you try to go in with the assumption that the boss is not consciously treating you like yesterday's garbage, that he's doing it because he is simply unaware. Who knows, that might be the case, and you'll find out soon enough. But going in with that positive attitude will help you to stay rational and calm.

Speak directly. Say what's on your mind—without a lot of emotion, just very matter-of-factly, almost Spock-like, giving specific incidents rather than talking in generalities. For example: "I'm assuming that you weren't aware of what you were doing, but when you called me sloppy in front of the group yesterday, it made me feel very angry and upset. In the future, I want you to call me in for a private conversation if you wish to criticize me. And I'd like for you to focus on performance, rather than attacking me personally."

Play tough. If the boss apologizes and changes her behavior, great. If not, reassess where things are. Often, says Jaffe, "just having spoken your mind may

"My business is hurting people."

—*Sugar Ray Robinson*

be enough to take you out of the victim role, and give you the ability to laugh off further attacks. If she's still insulting you, and you're still feeling sick to your stomach, it's time to go over the boss's head. Make an appointment with *her* boss."

Make your choice. If going above your boss's head doesn't yield positive results, it may be time to find a good therapist to help you deal with your emotions, and it's almost definitely time to start sending out your résumé.

CRUSH ON THE BOSS

GET TOUGH ON YOURSELF

Bosses. Either you hate them or love them. Sometimes, when the boss is of the opposite sex, and the two of you are working late into the moonlit-night, that love may get a little fleshy, tinged with romanticism and lust. It's called a crush.

A crush on the boss is never a good thing. It makes you liable to flirt, which can make the boss uncomfortable, create jealousy among your colleagues, and set you up for either rejection or an affair—either of which can damage esteem, career, and (if already wed) one or two marriages. Even if you keep the crush all to yourself, it still isn't a good thing. You're likely to wind up feeling jealous of others with whom the boss spends time or whom he or she bestows compliments, and that's potentially going to leave you angry and unable to excel at your job.

What to do about a crush on the boss? Here are some ideas.

Shift your attention. Don't get caught up in fantasies about you and the boss running together down a deserted beach. Such mindplay will only reinforce the attraction. When you find yourself drifting in that direction, take control of your thoughts and get them working on something else—like work.

Question your lust. Why do you find the boss so attractive? Is it that you're simply lonely and need someone to talk to? Is it the money and power? "Getting to the psychological base for your crush is often a way to defuse it," says Riki Robbins Jones, popular author and speaker, and expert on gender issues and social relations. Even if you don't defuse your crush, you can possibly rechannel it. "You discover you like his money and power? Fine. There are lots of other bosses in other offices that you can have a crush on," says Jones. "It doesn't have to be your boss."

Avoid closed doors. Try not to wind up alone with your boss. Chances are fair that he's already picked up on your vibes. One thing could easily lead to another. Avoid that for your sake—and his.

Keep your mouth shut. In some cases crushes are best acknowledged. For example, if you had a platonic, say, tennis partner, for whom you had feelings, you might want to talk it through. NOT with your boss, insists Jones. "Your crush on him is a personal problem. Your personal problem. And your relationship with him should be strictly professional. Keep it that way."

Run for the hills. If you absolutely can't get over your crush, consider transferring to another department. Find another legitimate reason to make the switch and tell others that's why you're moving ("I think I'd do a better job in marketing"). *Don't* tell them about your crush. It not only could lower others' respect for you, but they may also assume that the boss caused the problem. You could wind up jeopardizing his career for no other crime but that you found him irresistible. "That," says Jones, "wouldn't be quite fair."

DOING WHAT YOU LOVE

IT MAKES WALLOPING SENSE

The importance of choosing work that you enjoy isn't just some fluffy little piece of advice handed down by sweet old uncles at high school graduations. Those who've been around the business world know the truth: "If you don't love what you do, you'll never be successful," says Jane Applegate, popular syndicated columnist who has talked to over hundreds of businesspeople. "Quite simply, you're not going to put in the work needed to be successful if you have to drag yourself into the office every morning."

> **"You've got to be obsessed and stay obsessed."**
>
> *—John Irving*

That's true if you're running your own business, working as an independent professional, or ascending the corporate ladder. "I've met people who've made money doing stuff they don't enjoy, but it doesn't last," says Applegate. "All truly successful people get joy from what they do." She recounts having once written a story about a very successful funeral home. Did the family members who ran the business love embalming bodies? "No, I don't think so," chuckles Applegate—"but they absolutely loved being an integral part of their community and providing an important community service."

DUAL CAREER COUPLES

THREE MUSTS TO MAKE IT WORK

Once upon a time, couples fought about money, sex, and in-laws. They still do. But right up there as major sources of strife in many modern households are the eternal, nagging questions "Who's career is more important, yours or mine?"—and its counterpart—"Which one of us is going to make sure the domestic scene runs smoothly?"

Life as a dual career couple can be rough, often resulting in frequent quarrels, messy houses, and much ambivalence about going into the office (or coming home) some days. To smooth out the ups and downs and spare career and marriage, it helps to come to some basic agreements. Here are three musts:

> **"Never go to bed mad. Stay up and fight."**
>
> —*Phyllis Diller*

1. **Schedule time together.** If you both have hot careers, it's easy to get carried away and spend so little time with each other that eventually you become strangers. The way around it is to sit down regularly (say once a week) with both of your calendars and to actually designate specific hours that you will spend together. But don't just look at your weekly calendars—plan months ahead, if need be, so that you can be away on business trips at the same time.

2. **Run the house as a team.** "It helps to see the household as a corporation—one with no 'boy jobs' and no 'girl jobs,' " says Riki Robbins Jones. The two of you need to figure out what has to be done around the house, and how it can be split up equitably. Divide the labor so that each is doing what he or she likes best. If you both

hate, say, cutting the lawn, then hire someone to do it. "It's always best if you can schedule time when you're both doing housework," says Jones. "It's absolutely a lot easier to dust if someone else is vacuuming. If that someone else is sitting around playing computer games, or is out having fun, it often makes for resentment."

3. **Be clear on the BIG issue.** At some point in the lives of many career couples comes the ultimate crisis. He has an offer to go to Houston/Seattle/Paris that is the career opportunity of a lifetime. Unfortunately, it means she'll have to give up her job, and possibly put her career in cold storage. "It's real important to work out this issue beforehand," says Jones. "Tough as it is, you need to decide which career is more mobile. One of you has to say, 'I'll be willing to move if . . .'" Don't wait until the critical moment, or it could spell deep and lasting trouble.

SET PARAMETERS AND LIVE THEM

Two busy careers. One hectic relationship. Lunches, dinners, talks, sex—everything on the fly. There's no single trick to making it work, although some couples do seem to handle it.

"Dual-career relationships work best when both parties set out clear expectations for each other," says Judy Knight, a principal consultant with Oxford Training, an international management and consulting company based near Oxford, England, whose clients include Marks & Spencer, General Electric, and Volvo.

"For me, what's worked has been finding an understanding man who also has heavy work and travel commitments, but who has agreed that the weekends we spend together are precious," says Knight. "We also make sure to call each other during the day—especially when we have long days that roll into nights—just to 'check in.'"

EASING CAREER JITTERS

SEE IT BEFORE IT HAPPENS

Clammy palms, quick breath, dry mouth—symptoms of fear. Panic might grab you in the middle of a sales pitch, giving a presentation to a group of colleagues, asking for a raise, or simply meeting a big client for lunch and wondering how to make small talk. It may hamper your style; it may not. But it's never fun.

Much fear comes from facing the unknown, and one way of dealing with it is to not encounter the unknown. No, that doesn't mean giving up your marketing job to flip burgers. It means rehearsing and re-rehearsing situations in your mind until you feel comfortable with them. That's what some super-successful businesspeople say they do, including Virginia Littlejohn, CEO of The STAR Group, an international marketing and consulting firm.

> **"What, me worry?"**
>
> —*Alfred E. Neuman*

"The day before I'm about to make a presentation, I'll imagine myself making that presentation—and I'll see myself doing it from a centered place, feeling very relaxed and confident," she says. "You can get comfortable in any situation by first projecting yourself into that situation—and seeing things work out exactly the way you want them to."

HATING WORK

DO A THOROUGH AUDIT

There could be a zillion reasons you're miserable at work, but they tend to fall into two big categories—you either hate the *job*, or you hate the *career*. And it's essential, before you take any action, to get a handle on which one it is.

"To figure out why you're so unhappy, it helps to keep a log," says Rodney L. Lowman, a Houston-based psychologist specializing in work and career issues. "List everything at work that causes you grief. Try to make an entry every hour of the working day. And do it religiously for at least a couple of weeks. At the end of that time, analyze the list."

If, says Lowman, "your log contains regular mention of your boss, coworkers, pitiful salary, or your crummy little office with its view of the city dump, then you have a job problem." If, on the other hand, the list is less complete with specifics, but more rife with generalities ("today I just felt so incredibly bored"), that hints at a career mismatch.

Job problems can often be overcome by asserting yourself to affect changes at work, or if that doesn't fly, by looking for another job. Career problems are more complicated. "Most often with career mismatches, something, like perhaps creativity, is not getting expressed," says Lowman. "In some cases, a minor course change can bring fulfillment. In other cases, a major change, one that might require counseling, testing, and retraining, might be needed."

KEEPING PERSPECTIVE

COOL DOWN A BIT

"**W**hat ultimately sabotages a lot of people's success is—ironically—their panting after success," says Stewart Friedman, director of the leadership program at the University of Pennsylvania's Wharton School. Many people (especially young people) with no immediate place to move up in the corporation feel as though life's handed them a raw deal. "You somehow need to get through that anger and resentment. If you're mad because dad had it easier than you, you're not doing yourself any good—it will only fester and harm your health and career," says Friedman.

A better alternative to stewing: "Talk it out with your friends, your wife, a career consultant, or possibly a therapist," says Friedman. "If you can't get the promotion you want right away, realize that life is more than a career. That's not to say that we should all be at home constantly changing diapers." But rather—"invest in your continued learning and development as a human being, and think long-range about career growth and goals."

SET RATIONAL PRIORITIES

Are you always putting work first? Do you check your voicemail all weekend long, and sometimes even in the middle of the night? Are you more accessible to coworkers than to family and friends? If you answered yes to any of the above questions, than you may be a workaholic. Just like alcoholics, workaholics often deny that they have a problem—until it's often too late.

> **"Who loves ya, baby?"**
> —Kojak

"Don't plan on living next year—do it now," says Judy Knight, of Oxford Training. "If you're questioning whether to go into the office over the weekend or spend time with the family, ask yourself what difference your choice will make in a year, or five to ten years time," she suggests. "You'll realize that no one at work is likely to remember your task, but your son will remember that you didn't get to see him score in the big game."

If you can't seem to break the habit of workaholism, consider seeing a good therapist. Mental health experts say that the work-obsessed often wrap themselves in their labors to avoid dealing with some other parts of reality.

THINK LONG-TERM

Any career will have its ups and downs, times when you'll feel elated, and times when you'll feel let down, foiled, and disillusioned. "We've all been there," says Elizabeth Rogers, proprietor of First Opinion, a marketing consulting firm in Slough, England.

"When I am frustrated because a bid has not been accepted or the telephone has not been ringing, I have to think about the way a growing plant can convert rotting waste into beautiful flowers and sweet fruit," says Rogers. "This helps me to mentally pick myself up, look forward to some future success, and get on with sowing the seeds for it."

KIDS-N-CAREERS

JUGGLE WITH ALL YOU'VE GOT

You're a parent. You've got a career. Sometimes you resent your job because you can't spend more time with the family. Sometimes you resent the family because you can't spend more time at your career. In other words, you're human. And you're far from alone.

How do you juggle the two most important roles in your life so that both get fair treatment, and you don't drive yourself and your family crazy?

Set reasonable sights. Can you make it to the top of a Fortune 500 company while still being a parent who attends Little League games and school plays? No, probably not. The vast majority of big company CEOs are men with nonworking wives who do nearly all of the parenting. You can bet that those kids hardly know dad. That's reality. The reality is also that you can be an excellent parent and have a thriving career—though you won't head a billion-dollar company.

Don't cheat your children. The tendency for many is to put more time into career than into parenting. That's especially true of men who are conditioned at an early age to equate their self-esteem with income and job title. Don't kid yourself by saying that you can be a great parent as long as you spend "quality time," with the kids on Sunday afternoons. "It doesn't work that way," says Robert Jaffe, a Los Angeles-area psychotherapist. "'Quality time' is very important, but so is 'quantity time'—you can't separate the two," says Jaffe. "Children need to feel valued. They feel that a parent values them when that parent chooses to spend time with them."

Remember that little eyes are upon you. Your children watch you all the time, learn from you, try to emulate you. "You don't want them to grow up hating or fearing the notion of work," says Jaffe. Keep that in mind when you come home after a particularly rotten day at the office. "It's okay to express your feelings—*I felt so angry at my boss today*—but you should refrain from making such generalizations as *My bosses are a pack of slave drivers*, or *Work really stinks*," says Jaffe.

Accept the duality. Life as a parent and a careerist can be tough, but consider the alternatives. You wouldn't want a life of just work, nor would you want to be raising kids on welfare. Your career provides you with intellectual stimulation, a sense of accomplishment, and the money to buy nice clothes for the children and to one day perhaps send them off for a Harvard or Oxford education. Sure, it's going to be rough at times. "You need to give yourself permission to have that struggle, to know that you'll never do it perfectly," says Jaffe. "Have some empathy for yourself."

LOONY BOSSES

TELL 'EM WHAT THEY WANT TO HEAR

He wants you to be at the office around the clock, working, working, working. You, however, have another set of priorities, like occasionally getting to see family and friends. Crazy bosses are rampant in corporate America, and they make lots of people's lives utterly miserable. Dealing with them effectively is tough, but not impossible.

A typical employee's reaction when being asked to work into the evening goes something like "Gee, boss, I'd really love to, but I can't because my kid has a baseball game, and we have house guests, and. . . ." Forget it. He doesn't care. "The boss who wants you to live at the office obviously doesn't give a hoot about your interests, only her own," says Alan Weiss, founder and president of Summit Consulting Group, Inc., in Greenwich, Rhode Island. "To sway her, you need to address her interests and her interests alone." How?

> **"They are playing a game. They are playing at not playing a game. If I show them I see they are, I shall break the rules and they will punish me. I must play their game, of not seeing I see the game."**
>
> —R.D. Laing

Focus on what she focuses on: the work. Back to our scenario in which she wants you to stay till midnight to finish a certain project . . . You say: "Gee, boss, this is an important project, and I feel I should really give it my all. Look, why don't I work on this tomorrow morning, first thing, instead of attending the 9 a.m. marketing meeting. That way, I'll be good and fresh and can give this baby the full attention it deserves."

LEAVE THEM NO ROOM

Some bosses act like vacations are only meant for the weak, the slovenly, and the morally corrupt. These are obviously unhappy people, whose greatest desire is to see the rest of us become as miserable as they are. "You mustn't give them that opportunity," says Weiss. "With this kind of boss, you must never go in and ask if it's okay to take a vacation day. Instead, you need to FYI them by *very matter-of-factly* saying, "Oh, by the way, I'm taking two vacation days next Monday and Tuesday. I've talked to Sue, and she's going to be covering any slack. I'm certain everything will run smoothly."

MOMMY TRACKING

STAGE YOUR ESCAPE

Being a mom puts limits on the time you can (or want) to spend on your career. But some moms' (and even some dads') careers are dampened by bosses who figure that they can't be devoted parents and also be serious about their jobs. No matter how diligent, hardworking, or productive these people are, they won't get considered for promotion.

Unless they get smart.

Below, a few tips from those who have been on the mommy track and found ways to get off.

Make yourself seen. Most days you need to leave at 5 p.m. Fine. But don't advertise it. In fact, arrange it with your spouse or a babysitter so that at least once a week (on different days) you can stay

> **"The first duty of a revolutionary is to get away with it."**
> —*Abbie Hoffman*

late. Make certain that on those particular days you stop by the boss's office at 5:20 or 5:30 to ask her an "important" question. (If she's not there, leave a sticky.) "Yeah, I feel like this is a foolish game," says one mother/publishing executive, "but it wasn't me who set the rules."

Drop signals. Got a message for the boss? Make sure you leave her a voice mail or an e-mail, right before going to bed or as soon as you get up. She doesn't even have to know they're coming from home. She'll have the wonderfully hazy impression that you're working around the clock!

Be there when you're not. If you're working flextime or part-time, you don't want others complaining to the boss that they can't ever find you. Make sure your colleagues know what hours you are in, and what hours you are to be found "at your home office" (preferable to "working at home"). On off-days, check your voice mail at least twice for important messages.

Avoid the buzzwords. "Don't *ever* get up and leave a meeting at 5 p.m. because you need to pick up your child at day care," says one female attorney with a large law firm. "Get up and leave if you have no choice, yes, but tell your colleagues that you have 'an important appointment that you can't get out of.' Period." Similarly, instruct your secretary in the fine art of shading the truth. Instead of "Annette's at her son's school for a teacher meeting," she should say, "Annette had an early appointment; I expect her shortly." Also, ask your secretary to turn your computer on as soon as she comes in. Then, reward her handsomely on all the appropriate occasions.

Consider a car phone. It's a great way to stay in touch with the office or clients, even while you're running your kid to the pediatrician or soccer practice.

WORKING AT HOME

GOT TO BE YOUR OWN TOUGH BOSS

Working at home has its advantages, for sure. You won't have to dig the car out of snow. And if you like, you can work in your underwear. Or in nothing at all. On the flip side, you can wind up talking to yourself and eventually climbing the walls from loneliness. . . . Or perhaps lying in bed till noon, getting up only in time to watch *Bewitched*.

"The hurdles of isolation and lack of self-motivation can usually be jumped," says Rodney L. Lowman, a Houston-based psychologist specializing in work and career issues. But they are something to think about if you're considering giving telecommuting a try. For some personalities, doing certain jobs, the going may be easier than for others. But for nearly everyone, working at home will present challenges. Here are some ideas on how to meet them.

Build in social time. Lone wolf or social butterfly, all of us at least occasionally require human contact. "Build in your social contacts in a systematic way," suggests Lowman. "It could be a regular lunch date or at least something that you do every Saturday."

Create structure. Some jobs, like word processing, come in bits and pieces, each job requiring a finite amount of time and each with a fairly immediate deadline. Other jobs involve long-term projects with very amorphous midterm goals. In this case, says Lowman, "you may need a concrete plan for yourself, mapping out the project week-by-week or day-by-day." If, for instance, you have a project due in two months, plan on finishing roughly a quarter by the end of week two, half by the end of week four, etc.

Set clear boundaries. Sweet as it is to control your own daily destiny, it demands discipline. If you find yourself getting sucked into distractions like television, you may need to create firm hours during which you only work. Others in the household should be told that during those hours you are to be interrupted for tornadoes or nuclear war, nothing else. Some work-at-homers tend to labor too long, wreaking havoc on family life, even health. If you're a sucker for your work, you too need to set up a firm schedule for yourself—and let clients who call you at dinnertime know (politely) that you'd prefer they ring earlier.

Don't get sucked into cyberspace. Finding social interaction on the Net is okay—to a point. Beware, however. "The nature of computer interaction is such that there is a strong propensity for addictive behavior," says Lowman. "Some people are spending hours in chat forums, which can interfere with work and run up huge bills." Worse yet, he says, "Net surfing can become a substitute for human contact—satisfying to a point, but ultimately not a very good substitute for the real thing."

PANEL OF SHARP MINDS

Andre Alkiewicz is the founder and managing partner of Perception International, a Connecticut-based corporate consulting firm specializing in the early identification of political, social, economic, and technological changes. Alkiewicz formerly headed a Wall Street brokerage company and served as a British intelligence officer.

Sandra K. Allgeier is director of human resources for Providian Corporation, a financial services company with over 9,000 employees nationwide. She is based in Louisville, Kentucky.

Jane Applegate is a renowned business journalist whose syndicated column, *Succeeding in Small Business*, appears in dozens of newspapers nationwide and whose commentaries are often heard on radio and television. Applegate is a former business reporter for the *Los Angeles Times*. She is the author of *Jane Applegate's Strategies for Small Business Success*.

Susan Averett, Ph.D., teaches economics and business at Lafayette College in Easton, Pennsylvania.

Dave Barry is a nationally syndicated humor columnist and the author of more than a dozen of the funniest books ever written, including *Claw Your Way to the Top: How to Become the Head of a Major Corporation in Roughly a Week*.

Stanley Bing (a pseudonym) is a contributing editor and columnist at *Forbes* magazine, and the author of *Crazy Bosses: Spotting Them, Serving Them, Surviving Them*. He is also (under his real name) a senior executive for a large, multinational conglomerate, which he insists remain nameless.

Peter Blackford is director of the export division at Goodyear Tire & Rubber in Akron, Ohio.

Henry Bloch is chairman and cofounder of H & R Block, North America's largest tax preparer, presently with over 9,000 offices.

Gloria F. Boileau is a communications and image expert whose clients include Rolls Royce, Westinghouse, and the Internal Revenue Service. She is based in Cardiff-by-the-Sea, California.

G. Bruce Boyer is a professional-image consultant and the author of numerous fashion books, including *Eminently Suitable: The Elements of Style in Business Attire*.

Denis Boyles is the coauthor of *The Modern Man's Guide to Life: Advice & Information About Everything* and *Man's Life: The Complete Instructions*.

Wayne Brockbank is director of the strategic human resource planning executive program at the University of Michigan and consultant to Fortune 500 companies Dow Chemical, Texas Instruments, and Alcoa.

Marjorie Brody is president of Brody Communications, a training corporation specializing in business communications, based in Elkins Park, Pennsylvania. The firm's clients include Mack Truck, Johnson & Johnson, and Scott Paper. Brody is a popular speaker and the coauthor of *Climbing the Corporate Ladder* and *The Complete Business Etiquette Handbook*.

David J. Butcher is an accountant who runs his own outsourcing and consulting business in Lingfield, Surrey, England.

Mark A. Case is director of the career development office at the Yale School of Management. Prior to joining academia, Case had several years' experience in corporate recruiting within the banking and retail industries.

Holly Cherico is director of public relations and communications for the Council of Better Business Bureaus.

Mark Cipollini is the top manager of 61 Pottery Barn stores nationwide.

Theo Clarke is principal consultant with Tignosis Limited, a management consulting firm based in London, England, that specializes in cultural change and the introduction of new technologies. The firm's clients include National Westminster Bank, Exxon, and the Moroccan government. Clarke is also an executive director of SFC Press, a company serving the European hobby games market.

John Clizbe, Ph.D., is a senior partner with Nordli, Wilson Associates, a group of management and consulting psychologists based in Westborough, Massachusetts, and New Haven, Connecticut. He is also national chairman of disaster services for the American Red Cross.

Bruce Cryer is executive director of corporate programs at the Institute for HeartMath, a nonprofit think tank based in Boulder Creek, California. The institute specializes in innovative approaches to the problems of human stress, quality, creativity, and effectiveness. Its corporate clients include Levi Strauss & Co., Lockheed, and National Semiconductor.

Leslie A. Dach is executive vice president of consulting giant Edelman Public Relations Worldwide. He is the former communications director for the Dukakis presidential campaign.

Ken Daley is senior vice president/division executive with Chase Manhattan Bank.

Jeff Davidson is a certified management consultant, a professional speaker, and the author of 18 books, including *Breathing Space: Living & Working At a Comfortable Pace in a Sped-up Society*. He is based in Chapel Hill, North Carolina.

Mike Deblieux is a human resource and career consultant in Tustin, California, who has helped dozens of companies set up their employee appraisal programs.

Aviva Diamond is president of Blue Streak/A Communications Company, a Los Angeles-based firm offering training in media and relationships skills to corporate executives. Blue Streak's clients include Hewlett-Packard, Nissan, and Nintendo. Diamond is a former correspondent for ABC Network News and reporter for the *Miami Herald*.

Roger Dixon is a Toronto-based consultant on health and safety issues, whose clients include the Canadian government. He is a former vice-consul to the British Trade Development Office in the United States.

Edward Donley is former chairman and president of Air Products and Chemicals, Inc., a Fortune 500 supplier of industrial gases and chemicals, with operations in thirty countries and 15,000 employees. He is also the creator of six not-for-profit corporations devoted to improving education in the United States.

Kay duPont owns The Communication Connection, an Atlanta-based consulting company specializing in helping leaders in business and government to become better communicators. The firm's clients include Georgia Pacific, Scientific Atlanta, and the U.S. Secret Service.

Billie Wright Dziech is a professor at the University of Cincinnati and a popular speaker and writer on the subject of sexism and sexual harassment. Her books include *The Lecherous Professor: Sexual Harassment on Campus*.

Marsh Fisher is cofounder of Century 21 Real Estate, the world's largest real estate organization, and an acknowledged expert on franchising. He founded IdeaFisher Systems, Inc., a computer software company in Irvine, California, after selling Century 21 in 1977. He is the author of the *IdeaFisher: How to Land That "Big Idea"— and Other Secrets of Business Creativity*.

Bill Flister is a senior vice president/regional manager for Chase Manhattan Bank on Long Island.

Dan Fogel is director of the executive education program at the Joseph M. Katz Graduate School of Business at the University of Pittsburgh.

Eugene Fram is professor of marketing at the University of Rochester. He also serves as a consultant to numerous consumer and industrial firms and nonprofit organizations.

Stewart Friedman, Ph.D., is director of the leadership program at the University of Pennsylvania's Wharton School.

Catherine D. Fyock is president of Innovative Management Concepts, a Kentucky-based management consulting firm whose clients include Hardee's Food Systems, AT&T, and Hallmark. Fyock is former director of field human resources for Kentucky Fried Chicken Corporation. She is the author of *Get the Best: How to Recruit the People You Want.*

Joseph Goldberg is director of the Bureau of Consumer Protection with the Office of the Attorney General of the Commonwealth of Pennsylvania.

Eric Greenberg is director of management studies at the American Management Association. He is based in New York City.

Barry Greene is an associate partner with Andersen Consulting. Based in Philadelphia, Greene has done extensive consulting with such companies as E.I. DuPont De Nemours, Conrail, and Astra Merck, Inc.

Annmarie Hanlon is president of AHA Business Consultants, a group of corporate marketing advisors based in Lichfield, Staffordshire, England. She is also a volunteer consultant to the Prince's Youth Business Trust, an organization that offers coaching and funding to young entrepreneurs.

Gerald S. Held has been a Justice of the Supreme Court of the State of New York for the past 23 years.

Laura Henderson is president and CEO of Prospect Associates, a health communications and biomedical research firm, based in Rockville, Maryland. Prospect's clients include the Centers for Disease Control, Johnson & Johnson, Hoffmann-La Roche, and Apple Computer.

Roger Herman is a certified management consultant, business futurist, and popular speaker. He has authored five books, including *Keeping Good People* and *Turbulence: Challenges and Opportunities in the World of Work.* Herman is based in Fairlawn, Ohio.

Thomas Horton, university advisor at Stetson University in DeLand, Florida, is the former chair of the American Management Association and a former vice president of marketing and director of university relations for IBM.

Paul Jackson is director of Creating Results, Ltd., a holistic management consulting and training company based in Bath and Bristol, England. The firm's clients include Oxfam Campaigns and Hewlett-Packard.

Robert Jaffe, Ph.D., is a psychotherapist specializing in helping people who have been abused. Jaffe practices in Sherman Oaks, California.

Riki Robbins Jones, Ph.D., is an expert in gender issues and social relations and a popular author and speaker. Her books include *Negotiating Love: How Women and Men Can Resolve Their Differences* and *The Empowered Woman*. She lives in Alexandria, Virginia.

Jeffrey Kahn, M.D., is a psychiatrist and president of WorkPsych Associates, a management and mental health consulting firm. He is also past president of the Academy of Organization and Occupational Psychiatry and teaches on the faculty of Cornell University Medical College in New York City.

John W. Kennish, a former police officer and now a safety and security consultant based in Westbrook, Connecticut.

Sunder Kimatrai is the home office representative for Twentieth Century Fox in Bombay. He is responsible for the company's theatrical and home-video business throughout India.

Richard Kinnier, Ph.D., is an associate professor of counseling psychology at Arizona State University in Tempe.

Judy Knight is a principal consultant with Oxford Training, an international management and consulting company based near Oxford, England. The firm's clients include Marks & Spencer, Barclays Bank, The Mars Corporation, and Volvo.

Alfie Kohn is a popular lecturer, scholar, and the author of 5 books, including *No Contest: The Case Against Competition* and *Punished by Rewards: The Trouble with Gold Stars, Incentive Plans, A's, Praise and Other Bribes*. He has addressed managers at such companies as AT&T, Mattel, Pfizer, and BMW. Kohn lives in Cambridge, Massachusetts.

Roland J. Kushner, Ph.D., is an assistant professor of economics and business at Lafayette College in Easton, Pennsylvania. He is also a consultant to businesses, nonprofits, and government.

Thomas Leech is the principal of Thomas Leech & Associates, a presentations coaching and training firm based in San Diego, California. He is the author of *How to Prepare, Stage & Deliver Winning Presentations.*

Stuart Levine is CEO of Long Island-based Dale Carnegie & Associates, the popular people-skills training organization. He is the coauthor of *The Leader in You: How to Win Friends, Influence People, and Succeed in a Changing World.*

Virginia Littlejohn is CEO of The STAR Group, an international marketing and consulting firm specializing in the small business and women-owned business markets. STAR has U.S. offices in Washington, Los Angeles, and Omaha. Littlejohn has served as president or executive director of six associations, including the National Association of Women Business Owners.

Rodney L. Lowman, Ph.D., is director of The Development Laboratories, a Houston-based group of psychologists specializing in work and career issues. He is also an adjunct professor in the department of psychology at Rice University and serves on the consulting faculty of Duke University Medical School.

Clyde Lowstuter is cofounder of Robertson Lowstuter, a career development management firm based in Deerfield, Illinois. He is the coauthor of *Network Your Way to Your Next Job—Fast* and the creator and executive producer of *$ix-figure Networking,* an audiocassette learning system.

Michael W. Mercer, Ph.D., is a business psychologist with The Mercer Group in Barrington, Illinois. He is also a professional speaker and the author of numerous books, including *How Winners Do It: High Impact People Skills for Your Career Success.*

Barbara Oldridge is a marketing and management consultant based in Bucks, England.

Marvin C. Patton, is a retired major general and director of budget for the United States Air Force. Since leaving the armed services in 1982, General Patton has managed a construction business, a ranch, and an employment agency for temporary workers.

Colin Powell, is a retired four-star general of the United States Army and former chairman of the Joint Chiefs of Staff.

Alan Rappoport is president of Media Edge, a Beverly Hills-based consulting firm offering presentation skills coaching to top managers from companies such as Microsoft, Nintendo, and Compaq Computer. Rappoport is a former three-time Emmy Award-winning television news reporter.

Elaine Ré, Ph.D., is a popular speaker and trainer and president of Ré Associates, a New York-based management consulting firm with offices in London and Albuquerque, New Mexico. Dr. Ré leads corporate seminars on negotiations, power management, and communication techniques.

James Reinnoldt is Northwest Airlines' regional managing director for Southeast Asia and Greater China. Based in Singapore, he cofounded the Thailand Business Coalition on AIDS, a nonprofit organization helping the private sector deal with AIDS in the workplace. Reinnoldt is also a consultant to the United Nations World Health Organization on the issue of AIDS in the workplace.

Elizabeth Rogers is proprietor of First Opinion, a marketing consulting firm located in Slough, just west of London, England. The firm's clients include IBM Europe and the British Film Institute. Rogers has also authored several books on business, including *Creating Product Strategies*.

Craig Ronai is president of Ecologic, a consulting company specializing in the creation and operation of "green" businesses. Ecologic is based in Beverly Hills and New York City.

Lori Rosenkopf, Ph.D., is an assistant professor of management at The Wharton School of the University of Pennsylvania where she teaches a popular course entitled "Innovation, Change, and Entrepreneurial Management."

Carol Rudman, Ph.D., is a Long Island-based management development trainer who specializes in enhancing communication among all levels in corporations. Her clients include Motorola, AT&T, and American Express. She is the author of *Frames of Reference: How Men and Women Can Overcome Communication Barriers—and Increase Their Effectiveness at Work*.

Peter M. Saunders, Ph.D., is director of the Rauch Center for Business Communications at Lehigh University in Bethlehem, Pennsylvania. He has worked as a business communications consultant for such clients as Apple, IBM, and The Bank of Montreal.

Alec Sharp is an information systems consultant, educator, and speaker with Damex Consulting Group, Ltd., based in West Vancouver, British Columbia. The firm's clients include Intel, Kaiser-Permanente, and the State of California.

Dennis P. Slevin, Ph.D., is professor of business administration at the Joseph M. Katz Graduate School of Business at the University of Pittsburgh and management consultant to such companies as General Electric, Alcoa, and Westinghouse. He is the former CEO of four corporations, and the author of *The Whole Manager: How to Increase Your Professional and Personal Effectiveness*.

Clifton S. Sorrell Jr., is president and CEO of The Calvert Group, Ltd., a diversified investment management firm specializing in holdings of companies that make profits by solving global problems. Calvert is based in Bethesda, Maryland.

Robert Teufel is the president and chief operating officer of Rodale Press, Inc., a leading publisher of how-to books and magazines. Rodale is located in Emmaus, Pennsylvania.

Ian F. Traynor is a senior partner with Traynor, Kitching & Associates, a consulting firm that specializes in strategic marketing, business strategy, and the management of change. It is headquartered in York, England.

Robert Tusler is a consultant specializing in project risk management in information technology programs. A former executive with IBM UK, Tusler is based in Woking, Surrey, England.

Keith Weigelt, Ph.D., is an associate professor of management at The Wharton School of the University of Pennsylvania.

Alan Weiss, Ph.D., is president and founder of Summit Consulting Group, a Rhode Island-based firm specializing in management and organizational development. Summit's clients include Merck & Co., Hewlett-Packard, and Mercedes-Benz. Weiss is the author of numerous books, including *Managing for Peak Performance*.

Jon Weiss is executive director of the Center for Conflict Resolution, a not-for-profit organization founded by the Chicago Bar Association.

Stephanie Winston is founder and president of The Organizing Principle, a time-management consulting firm based in New York City. The firm's clients include Merck Pharmaceuticals, the Dictaphone Corporation, and the Discovery Channel. Winston is the author of numerous books, including *The Organized Executive* and *Stephanie Winston's Best Organizing Tips*.

Osamu Yamada is a writer of popular business books and magazine articles in Japan. He is currently the General Manager for WKKJ, a subsidiary in Japan of Hong Kong-based WKK, a manufacturer of electronic equipment. In the past, Yamada has worked with American Express, Sears, and Corning Glass Works.

Marcia Yudkin, Ph.D., is a Boston-based consultant and seminar leader. She is also the publisher of *The Creative Glow*, a bimonthly newsletter about making work more productive, and the author of five books, including *Six Steps to Free Publicity*, and *Smart Speaking*.